I'm Saved,
You're Saved—
Maybe

I'M SAVED, YOU'RE SAVED— *Maybe*

Jack Renard Pressau

JOHN KNOX PRESS
ATLANTA

Library of Congress Cataloging in Publication Data

Pressau, Jack Renard, 1933-
  I'm saved, you're saved—maybe.

  Includes bibliographical references and index.
  1. Salvation.   2. Christian life—Presbyterian
authors.   I. Title.
BT751.2.P73   248'.48'51   76-12401
ISBN 0-8042-0832-8

© 1977 John Knox Press
Second printing 1978

Printed in the United States of America

In honor of my mother,
Mary Jenkins Pressau,
and
in memory of my father,
Wilson Leo Pressau.

Acknowledgments

For the last four years this book has been my labor of labors. I'm glad it's done because I believe that what it says needs to be said now.

I wish to thank those who have contributed to the cause: my employer, Presbyterian College, which gave me a summer sabbatical for developing the ideas in this work; my wife and four children, who gave it some of "our" time and encouraged the author; the many student and other secretaries, especially Jan Needham who typed the final copy; the many friends and students who criticized portions or all of the manuscript, especially Lennart Pearson, our college's Head Librarian, whose suggestions were most productive; Richard Ray, director of John Knox, who guided the development of the book; and my wife Jane, who put her librarian skills to work in preparing the index.

Contents

I'm Saved,
You're Saved—
Maybe

Introduction

She says that she's saved and he's willing to admit that he's saved "if you *must* call it that." However, she's not sure about him and he thinks her attitude's juvenile. Frankly, *I* don't think the Spirit's touched either one of them.

Sound familiar? I imagine so. It is a scandal that the widest credibility gap among Christians is caused by the many meanings of this central doctrine of "the faith which was once for all delivered to the saints." It's ironic that the salvation understanding gap generates so much condescension and pride from some Christians and so much suspicion and ill will from others when *both* were exhorted to "love one another." It's tragic that many brokenhearted have not had the gospel preached to them and imprisoned souls are still in captivity because so much energy is used by Christian subgroups sizing each other up and saying, "I'm saved, you're saved—maybe."

I believe that a diagnosis of this disease more complex than "just sin" is long overdue and will be welcomed by Christians, lay and professional.

This book is a new, systematic, relatively simple and practical explanation of "I'm saved, you're saved—maybe." This interpretation lends dignity and offers cautions to each different *way* of thinking about and living one's salvation. Because it is theoretical, its principles are applied broadly as well as specifically to youth work, sermon illustrations, religious music, and Christian reactions to life's crises.

To taste this new approach fill out the Salvation Survey which introduces six understandings of salvation. Or, read through the brief story which makes up chapter 1. If either or both of these intrigue you, you'll enjoy what follows.

As you read this book the reasons why there are different concepts of salvation will be clarified. You can compare your personal view with others to see if you're in the majority or minority. And once you find where you and others stand, you can decide whether you like your position (or this system) and if you'd like to drop the last word from this book's title as you relate to other Christians.

1

SALVATION SURVEY

Which of the Christian views of salvation makes most sense to you? Read these views and their supporting verses and put a *star* by the one most compatible with your thinking.

Then place a check beside the two views which you think are held by most adolescents and adults in this country.

_____ Salvation is the most generous offer that there is. If you will honor God for a brief lifetime, Jesus will honor you before his Father for eternity.

"So every one who acknowledges me before men, I also will acknowledge before my Father who is in heaven; but whoever denies me before men, I also will deny before my Father who is in heaven."

Matt. 10:32-33

I consider that the sufferings of this present time are not worth comparing with the glory that is to be revealed to us.

Rom. 8:18

_____ As Christ created all that is, he has and is moving to reunite all that is into himself. The call of the gospel is to claim the personal and proclaim the universal salvation which already is by affirming and working with what God is doing and inviting others to do the same.

For in him all the fulness of God was pleased to dwell, and through him to reconcile to himself all things, whether on earth or in heaven, making peace by the blood of his cross.

Col. 1:19-20

For God has consigned all men to disobedience, that he may have mercy upon all.

Rom. 11:32

_____ To be saved means to identify with Christ in his life, death, and resurrection; to follow him as our perfect example and to follow mature Christians to the degree that they reflect Christ in themselves. To be saved also means that we join with the fellowship of those who have also accepted the forgiveness of sins and work, with them, for him.

For to this you have been called, because Christ also suffered for you, leaving you an example, that you should follow in his steps.

1 Pet. 2:21

Let us run with a perseverance the race that is set before us, looking to Jesus the pioneer and perfecter of our faith.

Heb. 12:1*b*-2*a*

Be imitators of me, as I am of Christ.

1 Cor. 11:1

_____ The religious impulse, seen in all peoples, accounts for different religions, including ours. We can see how others affirm their beliefs even as we proclaim Jesus. Likewise, we can see that all groups and nations have an equal claim on justice. Thus, "salvation" is incomplete until it focuses upon total peace between people and nations through the common denominator of all religions and humanistic philosophy: morality. Since leaders most affect justice and equity, we focus on them and the politics of power.

So Paul, standing in the middle of the Areopagus, said: "Men of Athens, I perceive that in every way you are very religious."

Acts 17:22

He shall judge between many peoples, and shall decide for strong nations afar off; and they shall beat their swords into plowshares, and their spears into pruning hooks; nation shall not lift up sword against nation, neither shall they learn war any more.

Micah 4:3

What is the transgression of Jacob? Is it not Samaria? And what is the sin of the house of Judah? Is it not Jerusalem?

Micah 1:5b

The threat of hell and the promise of heaven should always be held in the center of our attention. Salvation through Christ is the greatest relief that a person can know since his gift of peace keeps on giving throughout all of life and beyond.

"And do not fear those who kill the body but cannot kill the soul; rather fear him who can destroy both soul and body in hell."

Matt. 10:28

Do not be deceived; God is not mocked, for whatever a man sows, that he will also reap. For he who sows to his own flesh will from the flesh reap corruption; but he who sows to the Spirit will from the Spirit reap eternal life.

Gal. 6:7-8

"But he who endures to the end will be saved."

Matt. 24:13

"Come to me, all who labor and are heavy laden, and I will give you rest. Take my yoke upon you, and learn from me; for I am gentle and lowly in heart, and you will find rest for your souls For my yoke is easy, and my burden is light."

Matt. 11:28-30

Spiritual, like natural, laws are immutable. God's penalty for sin must be and has been paid. To be saved means to be acquitted from this penalty because the demands of God's justice and holiness have been met in Christ's sacrifice. Saved persons are "justified," seen as if they had never sinned in the first place.

Therefore, since we are justified by faith, we have peace with God through our Lord Jesus Christ.

Rom. 5:1

Then as one man's trespass led to condemnation for all men, so one man's act of righteousness leads to acquittal and life for all men.

Rom. 5:18

There is therefore now no condemnation for those who are in Christ Jesus. For the law of the Spirit of life in Christ Jesus has set me free from the law of sin and death.

Rom. 8:1-2

Part 1

The Bird's-Eye View

From Altar to Omega in Six Difficult Steps

When I was a child, I spoke like a child, I thought like a child, I reasoned like a child; when I became a man, I gave up childish ways.

1 Cor. 13:11

I

Once upon a time there was a very religious child named Pat. Pat was, with one possible exception, the most religious person in the second grade. That exception was Chris, Pat's best friend.

That spring Chris's church held a revival. Naturally Chris invited Pat to attend. The evangelist's description of heaven made it appear most attractive, especially for people who were older; but the description of hell made it seem like a place where no one at any age would ever want to be. So, when the preacher invited those who wanted to go to heaven to come forward, Pat was in the group.

Pat's parents said they were pleased by this decision, though they looked a bit pained when they said it. To commemorate the commitment though, they purchased a lovely Bible for their young convert. On the front cover, in gold letters, was engraved "Pat J. Long."

2

During the fifth grade an after-school Bible club was started in Pat's neighborhood. It was held in the recreation room of a neighbor's house. There were refreshments, games, Bible quizzes and drills, and a good time was usually had by all.

Pat was the oldest and brightest child in this club. This created a problem for the hostess, Mrs. Murray, because Pat began to win all the prizes. But Mrs. Murray was on her toes; she named Pat "Junior Leader" and "Score Keeper" for all activities.

Heaven and hell were graphically described at some of these meetings and the children were encouraged to "accept Jesus" in order to escape hell and gain heaven. It seemed that most of them were being frightened into their decisions. However, Pat thought of it in a different way now—it was God's good *deal*. Kids made all kinds of deals: they traded comic books, bubble gum, marbles, etc. They got together to do odd jobs each couldn't do alone. (To make more money than they could alone, they cooperated!) Salvation and heaven in return for the Christian life seemed like the deal of the century. Fair enough.

3

In junior high school, Pat's seventh-grade Sunday school class voted to become the communicant class of the church. The students studied with the assistant pastor from Christmas until Easter, preparing to "join the church." They studied the beliefs of the church, some of which made sense, and many of which were over Pat's head. But Pat liked the young minister and the ceremony was a moving and meaningful experience. Pat was now in an adult kind of way "numbered among God's people, a part of Christ's body, the church, for whom Christ had died." Pat felt very comfortable and content with these words the pastor used in the ceremony. To be saved now had moved from the just-God-and-me to the interpersonal: it meant to identify with the people of God.

Two years later Pat had another significant group experience. A non-denominational Christian youth organization had sent a team of young newlyweds to begin informal work near the high school. They were attractive leaders amd soon were holding informal meetings in several neighborhood homes. Many of Pat's friends belonged and virtually all of the big wheels attended: the jocks, the cheerleaders, etc. These programs attracted Pat too, who felt that this was the most significant Christian experience to date—it all came together here.

Pat's parents were puzzled and embarrassed about the attraction of this non-church group. Maybe it seemed more important than church because it was a group exclusively for young people. Maybe it was because the music, messages, and studies were youth-oriented. Perhaps it was the fantastic activities: the trips, the camps, the social events. Whatever it was, Pat felt more like a Christian now than ever before.

4

During the first year of college Pat became part of a non-denominational religious group for young people. In some ways it reminded Pat of the high school group, but there was a different emphasis—the nature and precision of your doctrinal beliefs. This made sense, though, because this was a group principally for college students, and in college you were supposed to learn how to think! And so, when the college group evangelized, it invited students not only to accept a person (Jesus), but a system of beliefs about him.

5

Because of a death in the family Pat had to drop out of college. The investment of three years of Pat's labors and some other helpful circumstances got the family business back on solid ground again. During this time Pat was cut loose from the college religious group and was given some leadership responsibilities by the church at home. This provided an opportunity to take a hard look at one's religious beliefs in light of the cold realities of personal and economic facts. At the end of it Pat decided that the religious commitment absorbed from family, neighborhood, church, and college was basically good, but left some questions unanswered. And so, with a sense of re-commitment to Christian growth, Pat returned to campus.

During the last two years of college Pat began to re-think the meaning of "the church." Perhaps it was because of the influence of the very popular and intellectual minister to students who had begun to work on the campus. Maybe the interim at home caused it. Perhaps Pat's switch to a philosophy major triggered it. Regardless of the cause, Pat developed a new view of "the church" and a new passion for ecumenism.

Pat now viewed the church from a spacelike point of objectivity. The church was Christ's body in many places, existing in different forms and traditions because of historical circumstance. But, because Christians were the mystical body, they were truly one, even though divided in so many ways. For the first time a concern for "dialogue" with persons of other Christian traditions was evident and old relevancies took second place—not that doctrinal precision was *un*important; but now it had to share Pat's personal priorities with ecumenism and one other new factor, social awareness.

By "social awareness" Pat meant an understanding of how economic, political, and religious systems affect people for good or ill. Part of Pat's new vision of evangelism (salvation) included the overcoming of sinful systems such as racism, paternalism, exploitation, famine, and poverty. This meant the cramming of a spectrum of social science courses into the senior year but, as Pat said, "How else can one intelligently focus one's Christian action toward the world God so loved?"

6

By age thirty-two our developing disciple had married, become a parent, held two jobs, and logged two years in a theological seminary.

With new inputs Pat's concept of salvation continued to evolve. In the theater of Pat's thought could be seen the drama of the human race. Creation was the beginning, the cross and empty tomb were still at the center, but now the history of humanity's struggle was portrayed as God working through people and nature toward their ultimate destiny and unity in Christ. As Pat put it in a paper:

> Jesus Christ, the Word, is the Alpha and the Omega point of our existence. Without him the universe would not have existed, would not have been redeemed, nor will it have a fulfillment. To be a Christian is to affirm and share in the agony of his re-creation through us. To evangelize means to share the good news of what he has done for and desires to do with us, and to work with all who have heard that Word.

> To affirm the Word of Life is to live the life of paradox. It is the most moral act that one can do; it is the ultimate non-negotiable, no matter how hard it is for the multitudes to understand. It is the most simple and profound, selfish and altruistic, natural and aberrant, subjective and objective experience of mortal existence.

As these words were being typed, Pat's six-year-old, Lynn, was walking down the aisle of the Christ's Kingdom Church with a school chum. The visiting evangelist, who was noted for his use of hellfire and damnation sermons, had just given the invitation to all who wished "to be saved from the fiery pit of hell to the safe and loving arms of the Lord Jesus" to come forward.

2 The Amateur Philosopher Who Runs Your Life

"Come now, let us reason together, says the LORD: though your sins are like scarlet, they shall be as white as snow; though they are red like crimson, they shall become like wool."

Is. 1:18

The prophet Isaiah and the psychologist Kohlberg both assert that everyone is a moral philosopher: there is a logical explanation for why each feels he or she "ought" or "ought not" to do something. Even when people do something immoral they try to justify it with some kind of moral argument or excuse. In other words, there is a kind of philosophical consistency to everyone's morality, good and bad. We often call this the person's "character."

To illustrate this point, let us use the most powerful method known to the science of learning—reader participation.

HOW MORAL IS YOUR DRIVING?

Here are six moral arguments for safe, within-the-speed-limits driving. Circle the one which best represents the morality of your driving.

A. "Drive safely; the life you save may be your own."

B. "Good" drivers drive at safe speeds.

C. Human life is sacred and must be protected by safe driving.

D. If you accept this driver's license you agree to accept whatever speed limits the state puts on the highways.

E. Many unsafe drivers get caught, fined, and/or put in jail.

F. The law says that you shall not exceed the posted speed limits.

After you've selected your argument for safe driving, put the letters representing these six arguments in the order of least to most mature morality. Do this here, or on a separate sheet of paper if you wish, but be sure to do it.

(Least mature morality) 1.

  2.

  3.

  4.

  5.

(Most mature morality) 6.

11

The Creative Dr. Kohlberg

Since the late 1950s, Lawrence Kohlberg, Professor of Education and Social Psychology at Harvard, has been studying the development of moral judgment and character. His principal method has been to present moral problems to males, ages 9-23, from locations all over the world.

One example of this "What would you do if . . .?" kind of approach goes something like this. "Assume that you are married and love your wife. One day you find out that she has a fatal disease. However, there is one very expensive cure for it, a drug available from the pharmacist who, after years of expensive research, discovered it. You cannot afford the drug nor can you raise the money for it by borrowing. The pharmacist will only sell it. What should you do and why?"

The "what" is not the focus because taking or stealing the drug is the only solution available, as most people view it. The "whys" or moral justifications, though, are where people differ. Some state that they would take it because if they didn't God or their father-in-law would punish them. This Kohlberg calls stage 1 thinking. At stage 2 the husband justifies his act by pointing out that he is, like the pharmacist, protecting his own (and his wife's) best interest. These two approaches Kohlberg classes together (he calls them Preconventional) because they share a common trait: selfish justification from the individual perspective.

At stage 3, justification would be, "I'm a husband" or I'm a ——————" (name of family or clan) and I'm doing what any self-respecting husband or family member would do. This is our way." At stage 4, a legalistic mindset comes into focus: "We swear to take care of each other" or "Marriage is a sacred part of the legal institutions of this society—and I'm protecting that." These two stages of reasoning are called "Conventional" because they are the way most adults in any society reason. Their common bond is that the *group*, whether it be family or political entity, with their traditions and laws, determines what's right and wrong.

A small percent of the population's reasoning goes beyond the Conventional Level: these final two stages are classed together as the "Postconventional Level." At stage 5, the husband realizes that laws are arbitrary: they are a network, a complex social contract among a people. The common "wealth" or good is the overall spirit of this code. Law, as Jesus taught, was made for humanity's benefit, not the reverse. Hence when a law puts property rights at odds with survival rights, society needs to re-think it. The husband feels that disobeying it is in order, either to protect the most basic human welfare (survival) or to "test" the law (push it to the Supreme Court), so that it will perform its function better. The spirit of the whole determines his reaction to the specifics.

Finally, stage 6 asserts that there are some things to which no human rules made by the few or the majority apply. The sacredness of life one of those situations. In stage 5 or 6 the person may add that he will steal the drug, administer it to his wife and then offer to pay on the installment plan or turn himself over to the law. There is an awareness that sometimes social contracts conflict and that until justice is built into law a person must follow a higher principle.[1]

Aphorisms

Our language has many moral sayings or aphorisms in it which fit the six stages of moral reasoning. Some of these are given in the following chart to give meaning to the Level and stage names associated with the system of moral reasoning Kohlberg found throughout the world—in countries with democratic and communistic forms of government, in highly civilized as well as very primitive tribes. If the readers cannot spot the correct sequence of answers for the "How Moral Is Your Driving?" quiz, these will be given in the brief commentary about each of the stages and Levels which follows the chart. The purpose of this commentary is to connect the moral stages with our everyday experience.

Preconventional Morality

Preconventional morality is illustrated at the first and second stages on the chart. Stage 1, punishment and obedience, is the moral assumption behind "big stick" diplomacy, people whose behavior is for sale (including pipers), and drivers whose sole control is that they may get caught and punished if they disobey the traffic laws. Letter E should be at number 1 on the quiz. What is impressive about this most primitive and childish Level is that so much of our behavior, especially driving, operates at its lower stage. The fact that the National Guard is called out in every severe natural disaster to keep people from looting is further evidence of the fact that the threat of punishment is the only thing which restrains many people from taking advantage of others. The Bible states that God and the state are the forces which restrain the outbreak of evil. St. Paul and other travelers appreciated the Pax Romana's safety.

The "Instrumental Relativist" second stage of Preconventional morality is a form of "enlightened self-interest." Persons reason that it is to their advantage to cooperate with other persons or with society's laws. The National Safety Council's slogan, "Drive Safely. The Life You Save May Be Your Own," puts the motivation to cooperate on a selfish basis. Number 2 on the quiz is A. The altruistic appeal, "Drive Safely, You Might Save Someone Else's Life," wouldn't work as well. The sign seen in some garages, "Poor maintenance is too expensive," asks car owners

KOHLBERG'S CLASSIFICATION OF MORAL DEVELOPMENT[2]

LEVEL	STAGE	ILLUSTRATIONS OF THE REASONING
I. Preconventional (environmental reward and punishment)	1. Punishment and Obedience (present and personal)	"He who pays the piper calls the tune." "Speak softly but carry a big stick."
	2. Instrumental Relativist ("I'll scratch your back if you scratch mine")	"Poor maintenance is too expensive." "Let's hang together or we'll all hang separately."
II. Conventional (group identified with gives reward and punishment)	3. Interpersonal Concordance ("good boy, nice girl")	"My country right or wrong." "Honk if you love Jesus."
	4. Law and Order (maintain the social order for *its* and our sake)	"When anyone's freedom is endangered, everyone's freedom is in jeopardy." "It's in the book."
III. Postconventional (autonomous or principled)	5. Social Contract, Legalistic (all groups, including mine, have equal rights)	"The president will uphold the Constitution, even the parts with which he disagrees." "We must play by the rules until they are changed."
	6. Universal Ethical Principle	The Bill of Rights, The Geneva Convention.

to cooperate with the mechanic's recommendation because the reward of now economies is less than the punishment of later expenses. Even the Revolutionary War aphorism, "Hang together or we'll all hang separately," doesn't appeal to group loyalty or to the revolution, but to concern for one's own long-range survival.

The Conventional Level

The lower stage (3) of this Level is called "Interpersonal Concordance." There is a shift from the selfish and personal to the group-selfish appeal. "Honk if you love Jesus" is a reminder to do what this group has determined is "good" behavior. "My country right or wrong" is an affirmation of a selective moral blindness when it comes to loyalty to your homeland. So is the appeal to obey the motor vehicle code because it's the kind of thing "we" "good drivers" do. B is number 3.

"The law says . . ." or "It's in the book . . ." are typical beginnings for the fourth stage, law and order moral appeals. Answer 4 should be F. It recognizes the danger of bias and so, at its best, provides an impartial set of rules for the "fair" treatment of all of the group's members. Its weakness is that the rules can become ends in and of themselves and do injustice to the exceptional case. Or people can use imperfect rules' loopholes to subvert justice. Some wag has observed that when Christians are obsessed with doing everything "decently and in order" (1 Cor. 14:40) and one of these has to be sacrificed, it will undoubtedly be the decency, not the laws or "order."

Postconventional Morality

Stage 5 "Social Contract, Legalistic" morality recognizes that rightness is often a matter of opinion and that human laws are not equivalent to God's revelation. Thus, it sees human laws as a set of agreements among the members of a society as to how they will live. Accordingly, the President swears to follow the Constitution regardless of his or her personal opinion. Number 5 should be answered D. There is nothing divine about a speed limit of 55 or 70. The laws are changed according to other considerations such as the abundance of fuel, the condition of the roads, or the technological level of the automobile. Our commitment is to agree to and follow whatever laws the majority favors. This perspective, then, being broader than allegiance to any law code in and of itself, breaks the bounds of loyalty to one's group, be it trade union, profession, or nation. It paves the way for the understanding of the world's workers and nations as groups of inter- rather than in-dependent peoples and countries. Perhaps it is the lowest level of survival morality in the age of the Bomb and the energy crunch.

"Universal Ethical Principle," stage 6, morality recognizes that even if 99.9% of the world's population agreed that permitting all Siamese twins to die at birth was legal and right, it would not necessarily make it so. There are some "self-evident" truths which must be recognized. Among these is the sacredness of life which we see expressed in our Bill of Rights and in the Geneva Convention. Score yourself correct if you put C for number 6.

"Touch all the bases in order!"

Just as baseball players have to touch first, second, and then third bases in that order, so all humans learn in an order: from the simple to the complex; from the individualistic to the group-selfish to the universal. This is the subject matter of "developmental" psychology.

Applied to human moral development, we observe with St. Paul that children think like children and adults like adults. Children tend to reason at the first two moral stages; adolescents and some adults are able to make stage 5 and 6 arguments.

Of course, we should not assume, because a person *can* make a good case at stage 5 for doing or not doing something, that he or she *will* act accordingly. In fact, research indicates that people can understand and argue at one moral stage above their typical behavior.[3] Nevertheless, moral understanding is an orderly or sequential pattern of change which can be observed if one asks the right questions. This can be demonstrated by asking a group of people of various ages to give you the best reason for driving according to the speed limits.

Intelligence Puts a Ceiling on Moral Reasoning Ability

The moral reasoning ability of a retardate would not be expected to be as high as that of a medical doctor. The reason is differing intelligence. Problems of greater complexity require higher levels of mental ability to sort out and solve them. Higher intelligence means the ability to reason at more complex levels. Thus, the moral reasoning levels of a society can be no higher than (and will probably be similar to) the distribution of its intelligence.

This was illustrated in a study of the moral reasoning levels of lower- and middle-class American fathers.[4] Both intelligence and moral reasoning tend to be distributed in a bell-shaped curve, that is, the majority of people are in the middle ranges and the minorities are at the extremes. In the six moral stages, however, the largest category in both social classes was 4, law and order, but the middle-class fathers had a higher representation in 5 and 6 while the lower classes dominated stage 1. One can see, then, that a political appeal based on law and order morality would have mass appeal!

Will You Please Get to the Point?

OK. From the human perspective, a person must decide to accept or reject the Christian faith on the basis of some moral reason, some "ought." Since moral reasons or appeals are at six stages, there should be six different understandings of, and appeals for, salvation. The appeal that will make the most "sense" to a person will be the one at (or most near) the stage where that person is functioning. Conversely, if the appeal is a stage or more below that Level, the person may feel condescension toward it; while if it is two or more stages above that Level, the person will not understand it and will probably find it threatening. So the evangelist's appeals in the tent meeting, on the university campus, or at the teen club will not only use different language and illustrations, but will be at different moral stages.

This raises a whole host of questions. Is there one or are there six stages (or three Levels) of acceptance of Christ? Is this Biblical? Does a person's reason for continuing to follow the Savior change as his or her moral understanding matures? And does it slip back when that morality regresses? Also, how do people interpret their former stages of Christ-commitments as they look back on them from higher moral stages?

These are important questions for pastors whose congregations may be characterized by a wide or narrow range of moral understanding. This is a key issue for parents who must decide to encourage or discourage their children when they are invited to attend various religious meetings, especially those of the youth evangelism organizations. Church boards that are asked to sponsor such an organization are faced with a similar decision.

For Christians concerned about the witness of the whole church this is also crucial. The criticism of one segment of the church in regard to the other's way of thinking about salvation is often uncharitable or even caustic. Ridicule and charges of "bad theology" or "heresy" are hurled. Is this justified, or is it evidence that "sin is couching at the door" and we haven't mastered it? The following three chapters will explore these questions "developmentally," one Level at a time.

Part **II**

The Worm's-Eye View

3 Me, Myself, and I

During the Advent Season, eleven-year-old Raymond was helping me place poinsettia plants in the chapel. While we worked, we were talking about the Christmas season and Ray articulated a rather profound thought: "I know what Christmas is all about. He sent Jesus to let us know that he wasn't out to smash us."[1]

As sure as our personal definition of "horizon" has us at its center, so our self is underneath everything we do. Whether we consider the psychopath's brutal disregard of the rights and feelings of everyone, or the death of a modern martyr such as Dag Hammarskjold who transcended his commitment to self and even his nation for the peace of the world, the self is always at the bottom of our behavior. The reason for this is simple: the self is where we all start. It is the common foundation level from which we build our human orientation. And, like the foundation of any house, we can always descend to it from the loftiest of its rooms: it's "downhill all the way."

The self, as such, is not evil. It's just built into our human nature, which God himself pronounced good. It's part of the equipment we need to live. Just as the lungs gulp air or we faint, suffer brain damage, or asphyxiate, so the infant hand clutches whatever goes into it. Just as the irritated eye reflexes shut and flushes itself when a foreign substance attacks it, so people all over the world search for heat when they are cold and cold when they are hot. Our bodies demand a rather narrow range of temperature, atmosphere, and sensory stimulation or we become irritable, irrational, ill, or expire. Thus the good physiology of survival translates into a psychology and a theology that begins with and is inevitably based on the self.

The real theological problem then is not the self, but our failure to transcend it at the correct times. This problem occurs because, when survival is no longer the primary human concern, we tend to search for greater and greater degrees of comfort, security, and pleasure. When the price is wrong, we sin.

This temptation to return to a selfish orientation when it is sinful is illustrated by the fifth Commandment. A command to "honor your mother and father" was rarely needed for infants and children of the Israelites—they were dependent upon their parents for survival itself. However, it was very much needed for those same Israelites when they were in the prime of life and were tempted to feel that caring for their aging parents was too great a burden (since those parents had nothing left to give them). In our day, when children are no longer the principal form of old-age security and "self" awareness and enhancement has become the pearl of great price, we see people who regress from self-transcendence and abandon responsibilities for both parents *and* children. Our genetic equipment will drive us to survive and satisfy our selves. We need such reminders as the fifth Commandment to check selfish impulses so that those of us who are responsible for both parents and children may not shirk those responsibilities.

Level I: The Self

Preconventional morality's total frame of reference is the self. "My pleasure right now regardless" is its earlier stage. The second and more mature stage differs in two respects: it is willing to *wait* for its reward and it is willing to *cooperate* with others to obtain its goal. But in both cases, the underlying motivation is that one "ought" to do a certain act with or without others because it will pay off and/or be pleasurable later.

Thus, the Commandment to honor parents is logically associated with this Level of moral awareness. "We took care of you when you were small and, therefore, you ought to take care of us when we are old." This is a kind of stage 2, I'll-do-this-for-you-if-you'll-do-that-for-me, argument. In fact, *if* the children of Israel did this, they could claim the promise of a long life (Eph. 6:2-3).

The very first stage of morality is implicit in this passage from the famous sermon "Sinners in the Hands of an Angry God" preached by the distinguished American theologian Jonathan Edwards in 1741:

> The God that holds you over the pit of hell, much as one holds a spider, or some loathsome insect over the fire, abhors you, and is dreadfully provoked: his wrath towards you burns like fire; he looks upon you as worthy of nothing else, but to be cast into the fire; he is of purer eyes than to bear to have you in his sight; you are ten thousand times more abominable in his eyes, than the most hateful venomous serpent is in ours. You have offended him infinitely more than ever a stubborn rebel did his prince; and yet it is nothing but his hand that holds you from falling into the fire every moment. It is to be ascribed to nothing else, that you did not go to hell the last night; that you were suffered to awake again in this world, after you closed your eyes to sleep. And there is no other reason to be given, why you have not dropped into hell since you arose in the morning, but that God's hand has held you up.

There is no other reason to be given why you have not gone to hell, since you sat here in the house of God, provoking his pure eyes by your sinful wicked manner of attending his solemn worship. Yea, there is nothing else that is to be given as a reason why you do not this very moment drop down into hell.[2]

To Be or Not to Be Defensive

Before some reader gets too defensive and begins to expend energy in pointing out that Edwards' "Sinners" sermon was not typical, and that there are many "higher" reasons for continuing to care for one's children and parents, etc., etc., let's face the central question of this book:

WHAT DETERMINES THE APPROPRIATE MORAL LEVEL OF A COMMANDMENT, TEACHING, OR SERMON: THE MORAL LEVEL OF THE GIVER, OR THE MORAL LEVEL OF THE RECEIVER?

If what has been said thus far upsets you, you probably sincerely believe that it is THE GIVER. I believe that it is THE RECEIVER. Edwards was a learned man who was able to think at many moral Levels—but what was the Level of moral understanding of the congregation who first heard the "Sinners" sermon? In regard to the fifth Commandment, the issue is not so much, "What was the moral Level of Moses' (or God's) understanding?" but "What was the Level of the children of Israel in the desert?"

Like a good teacher God communicates the gospel to us at our Level of moral understanding; therefore, we should expect that there will be appeals for faith at the selfish Preconventional moral Level, which is:

Stage 1. People ought to do what rewards them now or soon.
People ought not to do what will cause them to be punished now or soon.

Stage 2. People ought to put off short term rewards for greater ones later.
People ought to cooperate with others, rather than do what they want, in order to receive greater benefits.

These two stages may be illustrated by slogans which have, respectively, stage 1 and stage 2 moral appeals in them. The first is often seen on roadside signs in certain rural areas, "Come to Jesus or Go to Hell!" The second was often in the middle-class media some years back: "The Family That Prays Together Stays Together."

Who All Think Preconventionally?

Since moral understanding is a developmental matter, there are three groups whose thinking fits this Level:

1. Those passing through this Level;
2. Those limited to this Level;
3. Those returning to this Level.

As will be shown, this Level covers quite a wide range of ages and kinds of people.

"Jus' passin' through. . ."

All children start by being selfish in their moral outlook: the vast majority move on to group commitment or Conventional morality. Thus, we can expect that if an attempt is made to evangelize children, the appeal will be made at the "What's in it for me?" Level. And it is, at least by the organization whose single purpose is the salvation of children: International Child Evangelism.

Mr. and Mrs. J. Irvin Overholtzer founded ICE in 1936 on the thesis that children can and should be evangelized. Enough committed people have agreed with ICE to enable it currently to field workers in every state in the Union and in over sixty foreign countries. In 1975 it moved its 100-person staff from Grand Rapids, Michigan, to Warrenton, Missouri. There it now operates from a 660-acre former Catholic seminary complex. Price: about two million dollars.[3] This independent organization is part of a network of fundamentalist mission boards, churches, denominations, and individuals who believe and serve and give.

The basic program of Child Evangelism is the Good News Club, a weekly, after-school meeting held for children, typically by volunteers, in their homes. Perhaps its best known program piece is *The Wordless Book*, composed of five pages, each of a different color. The strong colors and the "wordlessness" capture the youngsters' attention. There is a leader's guide which contains the story that is to be told as the pages are turned. It is the story of salvation, by the colors.

Page 1 is gold. After eliciting the children's associations with gold, the storyteller gives a description of the place God has prepared for his children, a place where the streets are paved with gold. It's one where there is no sorrow, problems, pains, or crying. Before the page is turned, the children are to be asked if they would like to go to heaven someday.

The second page is black. There is no reference to "black is beautiful" because black stands for sin. Sin is what keeps people from heaven. The children are asked if they've done such things as fibbing, being naughty, etc., which are sins. Most answer in the affirmative. Red comes to the rescue because it represents the blood of Jesus, whom God sent to free us from sin. If we accept him our sins will be as "white as snow" (page 4) and we will begin the process of growth (page 5: green) as Christians. This story sets the stage for the appeal to accept Christ.

The Level I appeal for salvation is found in the Missiongrams, Tellgrams, Waygrams, Salvation songbooks, flannelboard stories, contests, puzzles, and other materials and program suggestions found in ICE media. After allowances have been made for the excitement of the club program, the interest of the leaders, and the quality of the materials, its success still hinges on a message that fits the audience. Children "read" wordless books because that story is at their moral Level: the carrot and the stick and God's good deal. If an evangelistic appeal is going to be made, this Level is the one at which it will make most sense.

"Stayin' a little longer than usual"

The moral development of some groups is late: typically, these people are called "culturally deprived" or "disadvantaged" because their intellectual, moral, and cultural development is behind that of others their age.

The moral Level at which the gospel is aimed for many of these folks is the same as that used by International Child Evangelism with "normal" (the right stage at the right age) children. An illustration of it is a comic book tract produced by Life Messengers for evangelistic work with teenagers: the story of *Ronnie Reb*![4]

Ronnie is a hippie. His problem is graphically traced back to Adam and Eve, who are pictured in the garden with a snake in the background saying, "He, He, He, He." Each page has a picture of Ronnie's slide into sin with a bit of dialogue (always in capital letters) and one or more related Bible verses and/or citations. The trip to the city costs Ronnie all his money and he ends up hooked on dope while, at the same time, feeling empty inside.

Ronnie's hallucination, during one bad trip, is a serpent coiled around him, looking at him eye-to-eye, saying, "Welcome to hell, small fry!" The picture on the following page is the snake's open mouth, drooling over the fires of hell, socking it to Ronnie: "Glad you could make our party! It's going to last forever." At the end of the story Ronnie is left still rejecting the exhortation of his Christian friend to accept Jesus. The picture on the last page is of the super snake (who has a screaming person coiled up in its tail held over the fiery pit) looking at reader, still drooling, and saying, "He, He, He, He, He, He, what about you? You might be coming my way *tonight*!"

Most middle-class, morally Conventional Christians would find this approach ridiculous, funny, or bizarre. Nevertheless, many people of the lower socio-economic and cultural groups find it meaningful. Christians buy these comic books because they believe that they contain a valid message which the recipients will understand. If we evaluate these approaches from the bias of Conventional morality or aesthetics, they are weighed in the balance and found wanting. However, if we look through the eyes of the person who can only think of punishment-and-reward-now-or-soon, it may be valid. It may be God's way of respecting his creatures at the first developmental Level.

God's Eternal Children

We move our discussion from those who are passing through the first moral Level to those whose moral Level rarely permits them to move beyond the Preconventional: the mentally retarded.

About three out of every hundred Americans are retarded, meaning that the upper limit of their intelligence is that of an average (normal) twelve-year-old.[5] Age twelve has always had special significance in the Judeo-Christian tradition. That's the age when the Jewish youth normally becomes a son (Bar) or a daughter (Bas) of the covenant (Mitzvah). Protestants have also tended to place the "age of accountability" at this time of life. It is then that most Protestant youngsters are encouraged to "join the church." Intellectually, the teens are when "normal" children enter the highest stage of development in their thinking. They begin to be able to figure out all possible solutions to a problem, to consciously use deductive logic, and to abstract and form rules to solve whole classes of problems.[6] In other words, for the first time they begin to think like adults! By definition the retarded will never do adult, abstract thinking.

About 85% of the retardates are classified as "educable" (mental ages 8-12); this means that they can learn most of what is taught in the first six grades of school, and in many cases take care of themselves as wage earners, and take care of others as husbands and wives and parents. Roughly 11% of the retarded are "trainable" (mental ages 5-7). They function well under supervision, often in institutions. The remaining persons, the "nursing care" or profoundly retarded, have to be closely supervised for life.[7]

Harold Stubblefield, a chaplain to institutionalized retarded and a former pastor, suggests that there are four ways of approaching the religious consciousness of the retarded:

1. The retarded have neither religious consciousness nor responsibility.
2. The retarded have religious consciousness but not responsibility.
3. The retarded have religious consciousness and responsibility.

4. The retarded have religious consciousness and responsibility "relative to their mental and chronological development."[8]

Stubblefield's view, the fourth one above, is based on his observation that the trainable and educable conceptualize religious ideas. Their ideas of faith increase in quantity and complexity as their mental age increases, but they are almost always concrete.[9] Salvation from sin means refraining from doing certain sins which must be listed, be "concrete," such as not cursing, sassing, dancing, etc. The ability to explain the relationship of God to humanity is not evident.[10]

It is understandable that the educable retarded have a very personal, or "selfish," concept of why one should become a Christian. And it is not surprising that many of them seem to enjoy the most *individualistic* of country and western religious music, hymns, and gospel songs—the ones that talk about "Jesus and me." The major portion of their moral thinking, regarding salvation and everything else, would be at stages 1 and 2: reward and punishment and "I'll be good for you if you're good for me."*

Those Returning to This Level

This brings us to the third type of person whose moral Level is Preconditional: the one who has gone beyond it, but has returned. What usually causes people who have transcended primitive morality to regress is a survival situation. There are many of these. A few will suffice to make the point.

Through the Valley of the Kwai is an excellent case study in moral regression and then transcending. Ernest Gordon is the storyteller. He was one of many Allied soldiers captured in World War II and forced to labor for the enemy. His lot was to help build a rail link between the railroad running from Singapore to Bangkok and the Burma line—through the valley of the Kwai.

As the men were worked to death they degenerated. To steal was to survive . . . even at another prisoner's expense. To rob the dead of anything of value was commonplace. Survival demanded absolute selfishness—at least everyone thought so, except for a few martyrs who chose death to protect others. After the bridge was completed and the men were paid, the moral Level of the camp improved. The officers, who were paid more than the enlisted men, debated whether or not to use part of their pay to purchase food for the sick who received no pay.

*Because a person is classified as retarded doesn't mean that there is an absolute discrimination between that person and another who was almost classified as retarded (say, 1 or 2 points on an intellectual estimate.) It's not a precise designation as in the physical sciences. Thus, higher moral reasoning can appear among educables.

This met with a mixed reception: some grumbled; others openly opposed it. The objections still echoed the old ways of looking at things:

"My pay is my own, isn't it? I can do with it as I please."

"We're all in a tough spot; but I need everything I can get for myself."

"When the chips are down, it's a case of 'to hell with everyone else.' Too bad, but that's the way life is."

The rejoinder was, "We sink or swim together. We ought to realize that an officer's first responsibility is to his men, and ours are in a bad way. We must share what we have with them."[11]

This argument is between Level I (each person for himself) and Level II (the group ought to have everyone's loyalty). Fortunately Level II wins and brotherhood breaks out. The men are no longer ashamed of themselves in front of their captors. They act "civilized."

The Kwai chronicle is about how men are broken in body and morality by hard labor under terrible conditions. What is the gospel for such "broken" people? Gordon points out that those who tried religion to get them out of this nightmare soon gave it up (that's stage 1: reward now or soon). However, stage 2 would seem to make sense: if we're faithful now, we'll be rewarded later. The same was true for the American slave who was "tired of livin' and scared of dying." We think of the spirituals as "quaint" because of their view of crossin' over Jordan to the better land. But the overworked slaves, with only future hope, were blood brothers and sisters of the men slaving on the bridge in the valley of the Kwai. For them and all the men and women throughout the ages who have been broken in all the ingenious ways our race has discovered, I assert that Level I, stage 2, is their good news.

The Lord Is *My* Shepherd

The situation was not unusual for a pastor: I had been summoned to the deathbed of a Christian. In a way I was relieved. The months of terrible cancer-caused pain were about over. Her battle with pain had been an inspiring one. I had nothing but admiration. Drugs were only accepted as a last resort. Our conversations were always inclusive of loved ones, the church, and God's goodness in life and death. Today, though, was different. She had gone "out of her head," the family said. She didn't even know her own kin.

I hoped that I would be spared a "natural" death like *that* when I saw her. The normally poised woman was curled up in the fetal position. She was picking at real and imagined itches, mumbling incoherently, and staring into space. Though I had seen her several times a week for some months she did not acknowledge my presence when I entered that room even though we were alone and I greeted her by name.

I took her hand and began to read the 23rd Psalm. Halfway through she looked at me and said, "Jack, what's happening to me?" I had to answer, "I think you're dying and your whole body knows it. All of your systems are probably signaling 'panic.' I guess it's hard to keep control."

I started over again, reading to her as I had done many times before, this time with what I believed were the appropriate emphases. "The Lord is *my* shepherd; *I* shall not want. He maketh *me* to lie down in green pastures: he leadeth *me* beside the still waters. . . ." (KJV)

A fellow minister stands out in my memory for two reasons. One was his pride in the sophisticated level of theology he was able to preach. The other was his admission that when he was called to the dying he talked like a fundamentalist. This bothered him but he handled it through humor and condescension. It bothered me until I shifted the perspective of moral Level from the preacher to the preachee—and his or her situation at the moment.

"What saith the scriptures?"

Before writing off Level I morality because of its selfishness and crudeness, consider that God uses it in both the Old and New Testaments. For instance, the book of Judges is based on the "Deuteronomic formula" which asserts that when Israel was good, she knew peace and prosperity but when she sinned, punishment followed. That's a carrot-and-stick observation which they understood. And, though it's over-simplified, as the books of Job, Habakkuk, Ezekiel, et al. point out, there is basic truth in it. Generally speaking, when Israel was true to Jehovah and to herself, during the period of the Judges, enemies were less likely to overcome her.

The peasants Jesus addressed were as limited in their understanding as were many of the children of Israel in and fresh out of the wilderness. Thus, Jesus spoke to them of salvation as a reward, among other things, and hell as punishment for those who ignored and rejected God's offer of discipleship, that is, doing justly, loving mercy, and walking humbly with God. The parable of the rich man and Lazarus in Luke 16 acknowledged that the poor peasant stood little chance of economic justice in the short run. Nevertheless, God's wheels of justice turn slowly but surely. The *unrighteous* rich will get theirs just as the righteous poor will also get theirs.

Much of the spiritualizing of this simple or "crude" message is the result of the discomfort of Conventional folk with Preconventional, selfish moral justice. Just because it doesn't apply to our situation doesn't mean that it didn't apply to theirs. Just because it's simple and selfish doesn't mean it's wrong. Nor does it license anyone to make fun of or patronize these people. . . . God is a respecter of all persons (1 Pet. 1:17, KJV). The gospel fits everyone.

Jesus Loves *Me*

The song most identified with child and Sunday School religion came from an 1860 novel. Little Johnny Fax is dying. As his Sunday School teacher walks back and forth with the frail child in his arms he is asked to sing. He does—a new song:

> Jesus loves me, this I know,
> For the Bible tells me so;
> Little ones to him belong,
> They are weak but he is strong.
>
> Jesus loves me—he who died,
> Heaven's gate to open wide;
> He will wash away my sin,
> Let his little child come in.
>
> Jesus loves me, loves me still,
> Though I'm very weak and ill;
> From his shining throne on high,
> Comes to watch me where I lie.
>
> Jesus loves me—he will stay
> Close beside me all the way,
> Then his little child will take
> Up to heaven for his dear sake.

After some verses from Revelation Johnny dies.[12]

This seems terribly melodramatic in the age of antibiotics and intensive care units. But in the mid-1800s, when the minister baptised the infant and prayed, "bring him safely through the perils of childhood," the parents knew that the odds were about 1 in 5 that their baby wouldn't make it to what the minister continued to pray about next: "Deliver him from the temptations of youth."[13] Thus, for the Sunday School scholar who experienced the death and burial of persons of all ages from the home, the grim (to us) middle verses of "Jesus Loves Me" were probably very comforting.

Touché

The story is told that when Karl Barth of Switzerland had concluded a series of lectures in Chicago, he was asked an apparently impossible question. Dr. Barth had been considered one of the greatest theologians in the world for some years, had set forth his theological position in the exhaustive, multi-volumed *Church Dogmatics,* and during the lecture had gone to great lengths to show the complexities and majesty of God's workings. In the question-and-answer period following the lecture a young seminary student took his one opportunity to ask the distinguished Doctor, "Could you sum up in a sentence or two the essence of your theological position?" The question embarrassed many in the audience because it appeared inane as well as impossible. After a moment's reflection Dr. Barth replied with a twinkle in his eye, "Yes, I could, in the words of a song which my mother taught me some years ago: 'Jesus loves me, this I know, for the Bible tells me so'!"

We, Ourselves, and Us

But as thrilling as it has been to belong to these great teams, I am more thrilled to be on the greatest team of all, the Christian team. Championships will soon be forgotten. Trophies grow tarnished and old. But the Christian team will go on to greater and greater victories in Christ.[1]

Have you heard of the Four Spiritual Laws?[2]

Stage 3

When most children become teenagers, their moral thinking enters the Conventional Level. At this stage the *group* defines "good" and "bad." The group may be the family, gang, team, church, organization, nation, etc. The earlier of Conventional morality's stages (Interpersonal Concordance) often goes by the cliché "good boy, nice girl." If "all" the girls are wearing purple socks to school it would be tragic not to. If "every" guy decides on a certain type of leather wristwatch band, then Junior will even spend his allowance on one if necessary.

Parents not only observe the power of peer pressure, but the influence of heroes or "idols." So does society. Hero endorsement of a product pays the company and the star. Prospective backers of a political aspirant evaluate the candidate's potential "image" before betting on his or her future. Every student knows that the "chiefs" have more influence than the Indians.

When the child becomes a teenager and shifts moral orientation from self to group it is good news and bad. First the good. It is a sign of growth to become less selfish individually. This is the prerequisite for lasting friendships (and who wants a friendless son or daughter?) and, later, marriage. But the new influence, friend- or group-selfishness, is also bad news. It is one benchmark of control loss by the parent. And so parents indirectly engineer the kind of friends, heroes, and environment their teenagers have. They send them to scouts, church, camps, and any experience they can afford to produce skills and socialization (friendship development). The more desirable friends are invited on family trips, and ways are made for their youngsters to share in the family experiences of desirable family friends. Another way, especially popular in past

32

generations, was to give sons and daughters books about heroes worth emulating, as well as the devotional classics. Two of these classics have been especially significant:

The Imitation of Christ and In His Steps

For more than four centuries the chief manual of devotion for Christian lands was *The Imitation of Christ*, which is basically a stage 3 appeal for piety. More than fifty editions of this 15th-century work (attributed to the monk Thomas à Kempis) were published in the 19th century alone. According to *The World's Best Books*, published in 1953, the *Imitation* was the most translated religious book in the world other than the Bible.[3] It was "the" devotional classic. The first paragraph catapults Christ-the-model into the reader's thinking.

> He that followest Me, walketh not in darkness, saith the Lord. These are the words of Christ, by which we are admonished, how we ought to imitate His life and manners, if we would truly be enlightened and delivered from all blindness of heart. Let therefore our chiefest endeavor be, to meditate upon the life of Jesus Christ.[4]

Written for monks who were encouraged to "cheerfully and freely submit"[5] themselves to their Superior in everything, why should it appeal to Protestant and Catholic Christians for so long a period? One of the reasons could be that Christ-the-model is not only the moral stage of the thinking of young monks but of many Christians young and old!

The best-selling book in the United States, up until the mid-1950s, was Charles Monroe Sheldon's novel *In His Steps*. Published in 1897, it has sold an estimated eight million plus copies! By 1965 only four other books had sold more: Dr. Spock's 1946 baby book (19 million), a cookbook, a pocket atlas (11 million each), and the late Grace Metalious's 1956 novel, which spun off a TV series, *Peyton Place* (almost 10 million).[6] *In His Steps* has had an incredible influence upon four generations of mostly Protestant Christians in America and throughout the world.

One of the reasons it sold well was that it sold cheap. Because the publisher of *In His Steps*, which first appeared in serial form in a religious weekly, only filed one copy instead of two with the copyright office, it was thrown into "Public Domain" from the start. An English publisher sold three million copies of the penny edition. The other reason is that it fit the moral stage of millions of Christians who have used the book's subtitle time after time in discussion of ethical decisions. That subtitle is *What Would Jesus Do?* The verse of Scripture which opens the book, from which the title is taken, is a Christ-the-model text: "For hereunto were ye called; because Christ also suffered for you, leaving you an example, that ye should follow his steps."[7] The book is a melodramatic explication of what happens when a congregation takes the example theory of the atonement seriously. Sheldon captures the idealism of adolescent faith in this book, a faith whose *modus operandi* is to choose a hero and follow him or her.

Christ-the-Model: The Scriptures

Simplicity is the crux of Christ-the-model. Teachers in all disciplines know the superiority of "show me how to do it" over "tell me how to do it." In fact, there are many teachers who cannot explain why they do things as they do. But, because they can do them and others can watch, mimic them, and identify with them, their example is a potent teaching tool.

Commitment to Christ is frequently characterized this way in the New Testament. Jesus told the disciples to follow him by taking up their crosses, being servants, proclaimers, comforters, etc. 1 John 2:6 states that the Christian who "abides" in Christ "ought to walk in the same way in which he walked," while in the classic passage in Hebrews 12:2 Christians are told to lock their eyes upon Jesus who is the "author," "pioneer," or "leader," as well as the "perfecter" of our faith. Later they are exhorted not to give in to exhaustion or persecution but to remain steadfast in this walk. Paul's classic identification statement is 1 Corinthians 11:1: Paul instructs the Corinthian Christians, whose range of behavior was quite extreme, to "Be imitators of me, as I am of Christ."

Training *vs* Education

Trade or training schools inspired the slogan used by the first Protestant youth group of significant proportion: Christian Endeavor. "No impression without expression," they asserted. Thus, Christian Endeavor "trained" and still trains youth to learn Bible verses, give testimonies, pray, and do acts of compassion. In 1881 education was far more concerned with theory than practice. "Why?" had a higher place than "how?" Then Congregational minister Francis E. Clark's brainstorm to "show" rather than just "tell" caught fire. In less than 30 years the Young People's Society of Christian Endeavor had 3½ million members![8] It was a religious "learning by doing" ("deweying") that preceded John Dewey.

Those religious youth organizations which appear to be the strongest are still the ones that emphasize "doing" and "following" over theorizing. The ones discussed below will be non-denominational but it should not be forgotten that Church Training, one Sunday evening program for youth and adults in America's largest denomination, was originally called "Training Union." "Training" and "Union" are terms going back to the turn of the century when most of the country was organized into "unions" or county units of the Sunday School and Christian Endeavor, both of which emphasized doing.

Young Life (YL)

Seminary student Jim Rayburn discovered the Young Life formula after the failure of his after-school Miracle Book Club. Assigned by a Presbyterian church to reach unreached teenagers for Christ, Jim realized that he would have to think teen in order to get and keep their attention. So, he

> resolved to accept their language, preferences, peculiarities, ways of thinking, and so on; to familiarize himself with their tradition, share their values, learn to speak their vernacular, and somehow move into their understanding.[9]

His formula was for the worker to be omnipresent with the high school set, win the friendship of the student leadership, get an even ratio of boys and girls to evening (not after-school) meetings in the informal atmosphere of someone's home (not a church), and there share in fun, songs, skits, discussion, and a talk. Fleshing out this approach are trips: to retreats, conferences, the beach, etc.—all neat places where people can share themselves and their faith without pressure for conversion.

Young Life, incorporated in 1941, is a formidable organization. It has well over 400 staffers and has attracted big money from individuals and at least one foundation, which gave it a million dollars.[10]

YL: Good Boy, Nice Girl

Conventional morality's earlier stage (3) is morality by identification. YL has captured this developmental principle in its approach at several points.

1. Secondary Modeling.

The key person in YL is the attractive not-long-out-of-college, sacrificing (there's no big money in it) Christian leader. These are people with whom youth identify before they move on to identify with Christ. As a YL leader put it

> "our critics point out as a weakness of our work that we are leader-centered. We shake our heads in some bafflement at this, because that's our greatest source of strength."[11]

2. Tertiary Modeling.

Missionaries found it more efficient to win the tribal chief first. This gave them an automatic hearing with the natives.[12] Likewise, YL realizes that in the teenage jungle (if I may carry the figure further) there are leaders and followers. I call this "tertiary" or thirdhand modeling. The high school hero (first) is a model who lets the YL worker model (second) reflect the light of (third) our primary model, Jesus Christ.

3. A Simple Integration of Faith.

Since YL is non-sectarian it must avoid any doctrinal or sacramental peculiarities.[13] Thus, the call to salvation is a basic affirmation of the gospel, and support to grow in depth of commitment. This "simple integration," some critics assert, cannot stand the test of the more sophisticated thinking found when the youth goes to college. However, the point is that ideology is secondary in influence; identification is primary.

4. Channelled Rebellion.

Some psychologies assert that adolescents in advanced societies have to rebel. So does YL.[14] YL, being outside the "church" as the teenager thinks of it, is a means of re-channeling religious devotion. It does not give the appearance of being controlled by the older generation (whose money actually supports the program) since the worker is the visible contact. So Sam and Sally Teen can have their rebellion and their parents can channel it, too.

In summary, Young Life is a dynamic organization which presents salvation at stage 3: Christ and his disciples as models.

"Jocks for Jesus"

Athletic imagery is not foreign to the Bible. The psalmist says that the rising of the sun is like the emotion of the strong man running a race or a bridegroom leaving the bridal chamber (Ps. 19:5). The dour preacher points out that because of chance or fate, and the times, the race is not always to the swift, etc. (Eccles. 9:11). In 1 Corinthians 9:24-27 Paul uses imagery familiar to his hearers who undoubtedly attended the Isthmian games. He exhorts them to live out their faith as if they were running a race in which only one could win the prize: an ivy or pine wreath. This green crown, he observes, is perishable, whereas the prize of the Christian life is imperishable. The Greek term for crown, *stephanos*, is used for Jesus' crown of thorns, the athletic prize wreath, and for the golden crown mentioned in Revelation. Paul also uses boxing to illustrate the absolute necessity of self-discipline in the Christian life. Hebrews 12:1 invites Christians to visualize themselves in the arena running the race of Christian life:

> Therefore, since we are surrounded by so great a cloud of witnesses, let us also lay aside every weight, and sin which clings so closely, and let us run with perseverance the race that is set before us.

The Biblical use of athletic imagery does not mandate or justify the organization of religious sports groups. However, it does indicate that athletics has been and still is a rich source of illustrative material for the Christian life because of its close parallel at many points.

What then does justify Christian athletic groups? The fact that star athletes have tremendous influence over young people. Advertisers use their endorsement to sell products to youth. Why not make the Christian commitment of athletes more visible to youngsters? Since teens follow heroes and emulate their stars, shouldn't the church set before its young and the world its best Christian models?

If morality at stage 3 is primarily a matter of modeling, then it is logical that the more models of exemplary Christian living the young see, the better the positive influence. Like Young Life's, this is a transference theory: identify with the attractive Christian whose life points to Christ, and then to Christ himself.

FCA

The Fellowship of Christian Athletes was conceived in 1954. Presbyterian minister Louis H. Evans, Sr. met with basketball coach Don McClanen and other interested laymen. Their dream: to "confront athletes and coaches, and through them the youth of the nation, with the challenge and adventure of accepting Jesus Christ as Savior and Lord, participating in His Church, and serving Him through our vocations." The baby was born the next year when Branch Rickey organized the funding of a year's budget. McClanen was the first executive director.[15]

With more than 75 employees, the FCA supports the activities of groups in 1,700 high schools and 300 colleges. In addition to banquets, breakfasts, and tournaments, FCA's focus is a series of summer conferences in which teens may come, play under, watch, and listen to big-time coaches and athletes. FCA's is a broad approach; it includes both Catholics and Protestants, the stars and the bench warmers of the younger set.[16]

FCA members are bombarded with witnesses to the faith through a book of devotions (each day's written by a name athlete), films and filmstrips, tapes and a record (entitled "Under the Master Coach"), tracts, pins, T shirts, decals, and Bibles offered by the organization. They are all items of identification with a group which identifies itself with Christ.

A.I.A.

Athletes in Action is a johnny-come-lately subdivision of Campus Crusade for Christ. With a team of 200 staffers it draws young people to a variety of events through the lure of pros such as Brooks Robinson, Bob Pettit, and Bill Glass, who have also given their witness through FCA.

The *Time* writer criticizes both FCA and A.I.A.

> Some critics find a basic conflict between the aggression and ego worship of sports and authentic Christianity. Sports evangelism tends to worship success, although FCA, at least, also seems geared to the bench warmers of the world. Beyond that, most of the heavyweight preachers are theological lightweights . . . . But if FCA and A.I.A. teach a theologically thin, no-sweat Christianity, so do many churches these days.[17]

"Theologically thin" may mean gearing an appeal to the Christian faith on the basis of stage 3 morality. It is oversimplified *if* you compare it with stages 4, 5, and 6 but not with 1 or 2. Apparently the moral development of a large number of high school and college athletes (as well as many other folks) is stage 3.

Athletic images (and imagery), in our culture, are an excellent way to communicate the gospel at stage 3 to people of the Conventional moral Level. In itself, this is not bad. It is where Paul was, according to 2 Timothy 4:6-8, when he contemplated his own impending execution, still mixing the metaphors of running and boxing:

> For I am already on the point of being sacrificed; the time of my departure has come. I have fought the good fight, I have finished the race, I have kept the faith. Henceforth there is laid up for me the crown of righteousness, which the Lord, the righteous judge, will award to me on that Day, and not only to me but also to all who have loved his appearing.

Everything You Always AWANA-ed to Know

AWANA (*A*pproved *W*orkmen *A*re *N*ot *A*shamed, from 2 Tim. 2:15) is an independent evangelical scout-like program that churches may provide for youngsters in grades 3 through 12. Its target populations are the churched and unchurched youth of a church's neighborhood and their families. Its objectives are to provide a wholesome and Bible-centered weekday experience for the church's youth, training in Bible knowledge, doctrine, evangelism, and service. It is also to provide Christian models at a time when children and youth become influenced beyond the home. Purpose six is:

> Boys and girls need adult guidance in addition to that of parents and school teachers. The world offers its heroes who may lead minds and hearts away from things eternal. Awana Clubs provide leaders who point young folks to God and His Word. [18]

Chums and Pals are the names of the programs for girls and boys, respectively, in the third, fourth, and fifth grades. The motif is Indian. From sixth through eighth grades the girls become Guards, with a nautical program theme, while the boys become Pioneers, with western-type activities. Sex segregation ends in high school with the ninth- through twelfth-grade Shipmates program.

All the identity elements associated with scouting are provided by AWANA: charter, uniforms, regional events, awards, district workers, leadership training sessions, etc. In essence: AWANA channels youth's desire to join and identify, but keeps it in a church-identified organization. It is the most doctrinally specific of all the organizations mentioned thus far, as its statement makes clear:

> Awana upholds the fundamental doctrines of the Bible which is held to be verbally inspired; the three persons of the Godhead, Father, Son, and Holy Spirit; the virgin birth of Christ; His bodily resurrection; His coming again as premillennial; our condition as lost sinners; the need of being saved through faith in the finished work of Christ on Calvary, and that alone, without any works; the believer's walk of separation from the world; the believer's baptism by immersion in obedience to God's Word; the eternal happiness of the saved and eternal punishment of the lost. [19]

Stage 3, Summary

Interpersonal Concordance is the first stage of what is called "Conventional" (Level II) morality. Known as "good boy, nice girl," its religious name is "Christ(ian)-the-model" because the Christian hero and group become the means of directing a person's commitment eventually to Christ himself. Because the focus is on following, the ideology of the groups is generally limited and simple.

Two best-selling Christian books, *The Imitation of Christ* and *In His Steps*, are aimed primarily at this Level of thinking. Three types of youth organizations also appear to function principally at this Level: youth evangelism as illustrated by Young Life (Youth for Christ is another example), youth athletic evangelistic groups like FCA and A.I.A., and an evangelical substitute for Boy and Girl Scouts: AWANA. The view of the atonement most compatible with this is called the "example" theory—Christ died for us and he set us an example of how to live through his own sinless life and through the examples of his saints, especially those whom Christian people most respect.

Stage 4: Law and Order

When Junior marries, mother doesn't lose a son, she gains a daughter. Likewise, when Junior moves to stage 4 in his moral development, he doesn't lose group- and hero-loyalty, he gains an ideology to go with them. Group-loyalty and law and order go together: their union is called "Conventional," or Level II, morality.

"Law" here means a system of beliefs which fits neatly together. Since our focus is Christian commitment, it would be God's laws as understood and codified by the group to which one pledges allegiance. In this context "order" could refer to the enforcement of "lawful" behavior. Formal groups, like churches, have spelled out procedures to discipline erring ministers or deviant congregations. Informal groups use more subtle methods to keep members in line like shunning (withdrawal of emotional support and approval), rebuke, and condemnation.

This moral stage fits one of the dominant views of salvation: the "legal" view—propounded, not surprisingly, by a lawyer, Grotius. According to this view, God's law is an extension of his will which is set apart from him just as laws of a country (the will of its people expressed through their legislature's actions) are set apart from its people. Humans broke this law. Justice must be satisfied. That's what the cross accomplished when Christ was punished in our place.

Campus Crusade for Christ

With stage 3 Christ(ian)-the-model style, Dr. William R. Bright leads an evangelistic organization of well over 3,000 paid workers plus many more volunteers whose goal is to evangelize academia by 1976 and the world by 1980![20] Their major device is a booklet which contains a set of stage 4, law and order, principles that appeal to the legal mindset: *Have You Heard of the Four Spiritual Laws?*[21] Millions of these have been distributed in conversations, interviews, group meetings, and through follow-ups to telephone "surveys."[22]

Campus Crusade for Christ, like Young Life, emphasizes both staff and volunteer training. Evangelizers are given countless strategies for getting a person to listen to a Scripture-verse-supported presentation of

Have You Heard of the Four Spiritual Laws?

Just as there are physical laws that govern the physical universe, so are there spiritual laws which govern your relationship with God.

LAW ONE

GOD **LOVES** YOU, AND HAS A WONDERFUL **PLAN** FOR YOUR LIFE.

GOD'S LOVE

"For God so loved the world, that He gave His only begotten Son, that whoever believes in Him should not perish, but have eternal life" (John 3:16).

GOD'S PLAN

(Christ speaking) "I came that they might have life, and might have it abundantly" (that it might be full and meaningful) (John 10:10).

Why is it that most people are not experiencing the abundant life?

Because

LAW TWO

MAN IS **SINFUL** AND **SEPARATED** FROM GOD, THUS HE CANNOT KNOW AND EXPERIENCE GOD'S LOVE AND PLAN FOR HIS LIFE.

MAN IS SINFUL

"For all have sinned and fall short of the glory of God" (Romans 3:23).

Man was created to have fellowship with God; but, because of his own stubborn self-will, he chose to go his own independent way and fellowship with God was broken. This self-will, characterized by an attitude of active rebellion or passive indifference, is an evidence of what the Bible calls sin.

MAN IS SEPARATED

"For the wages of sin is death" (spiritual separation from God) (Romans 6:23).

God is holy and man is sinful. A great chasm separates the two. Man is continually trying to reach God and the abundant life through his own efforts: good life, ethics, philosophy, etc.

The Third Law gives us the only answer to this dilemma...

LAW THREE

JESUS CHRIST IS GOD'S **ONLY** PROVISION FOR MAN'S SIN. THROUGH HIM YOU CAN KNOW AND EXPERIENCE GOD'S LOVE AND PLAN FOR YOUR LIFE.

HE DIED IN OUR PLACE

"But God demonstrates His own love toward us, in that while we were yet sinners, Christ died for us" (Romans 5:8).

HE ROSE FROM THE DEAD

"Christ died for our sins...He was buried...He was raised on the third day according to the Scriptures...He appeared to Cephas, then to the twelve. After that He appeared to more than five hundred..." (I Corinthians 15:3-6).

HE IS THE ONLY WAY

"Jesus said to him, 'I am the way, and the truth, and the life; no one comes to the Father, but through Me'" (John 14:6).

God has bridged the chasm which separates us from Him by sending His Son, Jesus Christ, to die on the cross in our place.

It is not enough just to know these three laws...

LAW FOUR

WE MUST INDIVIDUALLY **RECEIVE** JESUS CHRIST AS SAVIOR AND LORD; THEN WE CAN KNOW AND EXPERIENCE GOD'S LOVE AND PLAN FOR OUR LIVES.

WE MUST RECEIVE CHRIST

"But as many as received Him, to them He gave the right to become children of God, even to those who believe in His name" (John 1:12).

WE RECEIVE CHRIST THROUGH FAITH

"For by grace you have been saved through faith; and that not of yourselves, it is the gift of God; not as a result of works, that no one should boast" (Ephesians 2:8,9).

WE RECEIVE CHRIST BY PERSONAL INVITATION

(Christ is speaking): "Behold, I stand at the door and knock; if any one hears My voice and opens the door, I will come in to him" (Revelation 3:20).

Receiving Christ involves turning to God from self, trusting Christ to come into our lives, to forgive our sins and to make us what He wants us to be. It is not enough to give intellectual assent to His claims or to have an emotional experience.

These two circles represent two kinds of lives:

SELF-CONTROLLED LIFE

E—Ego or finite self on the throne
†—Christ outside the life
•—Interests controlled by self, often resulting in discord and frustration

CHRIST-CONTROLLED LIFE

†—Christ on the throne of the life
E—Ego—self dethroned
•—Interests under control of infinite God, resulting in harmony with God's plan

Which circle represents your life?
Which circle would you like to have represent your life?
The following explains how you can receive Christ:

YOU CAN RECEIVE CHRIST RIGHT NOW THROUGH PRAYER (Prayer is talking with God)

God knows your heart and is not so concerned with your words as He is with the attitude of your heart. The following is a suggested prayer:

"Lord Jesus, I need You. I open the door of my life and receive You as my Savior and Lord. Thank You for forgiving my sins. Take control of the throne of my life. Make me the kind of person You want me to be."

Does this prayer express the desire of your heart?

If it does, pray this prayer right now, and Christ will come into your life, as He promised.

the four laws. " 'Ours is a low-pressure approach, logical and practical,' " states Dr. Bright. " 'The approach is based on the idea that college students have a basic spiritual hunger and will respond if the claims of Christ are communicated simply by a spirit-controlled person.' "[23]

Since most students move into the stage 4 moral perspective during their college years, the legal or propositional invitation to Christ is most relevant to them. In fact the passion for a system which answers all questions of belief and practice typically peaks during mid to late adolescence. This is because the students' minds have developed to the place where they can now think in terms of a philosophy of all of life. A "plan" of salvation, then, can become the heart of their philosophy. Thus, Campus Crusade has a tremendous Conventional pull, in terms of its moral Level. It offers a stage 4 set of spiritual laws through the stage 3, Christ(ian)-the-model medium of attractive and committed young staff persons.

This orderly "plan of salvation" is an advanced form of the message of *The Wordless Book*, used by stage 1 and 2 International Child Evangelism mentioned in the last chapter. But here laws or rules are emphasized more than divine pleasure or anger. Furthermore, as one reads much CCC literature there are other systems the believer is exhorted to follow (such as the "Sound Mind Principle") each with "x" number of steps.[24] A former CCC worker was reported to have said that even though his theology was evangelical, his categories of thought had to be those of fundamentalism (classic stage 4 Christian thinking) or he was judged inadequate.[25] In other words, CCC is a typical Conventional morality movement because it demands adherence to a total system of beliefs (laws) and practices (orders) with which it (and the churches it judges to be "spiritual") concurs.[26]

Inter-Varsity Christian Fellowship (IVCF)

Campus Crusade was an outgrowth of Dr. and Mrs. Bright's work at U.C.L.A., which began in 1951. An older college and university evangelistic group (1939-40 in U.S.A., and 1920s in England and Canada) is Inter-Varsity. It is less leader-oriented and formula-minded than Campus Crusade. It is also less successful in terms of size of staff and visibility.

Robert S. Ellwood says that "Inter-Varsity presents what might be called an intellectual's evangelicalism."[27] IVCF leaves room for differences about the methods of evangelism and belies a focused placement at some moral stage. It undoubtedly leaves room for students to move from stage 4 and Conventional morality to a Postconventional moral orientation without ostracism. Some people cannot understand how a group can have intellectual and methodological freedom as well as evangelical passion. That IVCF has quietly accomplished this for decades is proved by the nature and quality of its most spectacular event: the Urbana Missionary Conference, held over alternate Christmas holidays. This meeting is a prime recruiting time for dozens of independent and denominational mission boards.

Basic Youth Conflicts Seminar

Bill Gothard is the architect and only lecturer of a traveling Institute which sets up 32-hour, six-day "seminars" in major cities at $35 to $45 per listener. Using no paid advertising, just word-of-mouth and the evangelical grapevine mainly, Gothard packs the house.[28] Though he began with only a handful of participants in 1967, over 50 thousand heard him in 1971, about 125 thousand in 1972, and over a quarter of a million in 1973! His organization, which has headquarters at Oak Brook, Illinois, had an 8 million dollar budget in 1974 and a home staff of over 70. At present his organization is also developing a curriculum for public and church schools.[29]

The Institute issues each one who attends a seminar a red notebook from which the attender is to study Gothard's comprehensive system of beliefs and directives (laws and orders) for Christian living. Participants are not to share its contents with non-attenders. The focus is on these relationships: persons to God, persons to themselves, and persons to other persons. Gothard's belief system focuses on the easily remembered "chain of command" principle and its classic illustration: The child is the diamond in the rough, the father is the hammer, and the mother is the chisel. God is pictured as using the hammer to direct the chisel to cut the stone into a beautiful gem. In other words, God directs father who directs mother who directs child. All is well when everyone is obedient to God's law.[30]

With earnestness to be devout Gothard gives his listeners checklists and solution systems. The ultimate purpose of this system is to answer *all* ethical questions in a way that is consistent with what Gothard terms "root problems." *The* root problem, though, is disobedience to God. Since the seminar is also for young attenders, Gothard's list of rules covers dating problems, rebellion, and other youth issues. This system of Christian behavior has made a profound impact upon thousands in spite of the fact that it is counter to most popular trends.[31] Andrew Wallace of the Philadelphia *Inquirer* (the newspaper) dubs this an "encyclopedia of Christian behavior."[32] Gothard is unashamed that it is an authoritative system. The authority acts as an "umbrella" of protection against satanic powers, he believes.[33]

Like Campus Crusade, the Institute's approach to person-to-person and family life is clearly pitched to stage 4 thinking. There is the authority of law, and the orderly procedure to follow in obeying laws or when the laws are broken. The "model" is a total system of laws which are believed to be divinely sanctioned. Thus, the founder asserts that the *whole* system must be judged rather than its parts.

Reprise and Observation

The readers are reminded that the vast majority of young people and adults are at stages 3 and 4, Conventional morality. The larger portion of adults are at stage 4. It should come as no surprise, then, that these successful (in terms of growth at least) programs have structured themselves in this fashion. For those who accept them they are exciting, meaningful, and reassuring. They are definitely evangelical. Most are fully compatible with the legal, forensic, or (as it's popularly known) "substitutionary" doctrine of the atonement. The question that stage theory raises is whether stage 4 salvation should be taught as:

1. a step along the way toward maturity;
2. a completely valid, mature system of belief; or
3. both.

5 The World, The Universe, ALL

"I have not come to destroy the law, but to fulfill it."
Jesus (Matt. 5:17, free translation)

In the present world context—where inter-faith consultations are the order—there are two major issues which post-Christian Western society may have started to formulate which now call for worldwide understanding and effective solutions. They are the new concern for the protection of our environment and the slightly older one of world justice and development.[1]

In Teilhard's theology of Redemption, Christ not only bears the sins of the world but also the weight of the world in evolution. For Teilhard, then, the Cross is the symbol not only of reparation and expiation but the symbol of the redemptive unification of the world, of the progress of the world toward Christ-Omega. The Cross is the symbol of the synthesis of the "upward" component of sacrifice and adoring reparation and the "forward" component of progress through laborious effort.[2]

The person who solves the most difficult moral problems will have to be very intelligent. This chapter is about such Christians, how they think of salvation and its moral implications.

One should not jump to the conclusion that because high intelligence is required for Postconventional moral judgment all bright people are moral. This line of reasoning is faulty in two ways. First, moral judgment is a specific kind of thinking. Just as some mathematicians and physicians never develop their musical or athletic potential, so some bright folks may have neglected their moral development. Second, because a person *can* do complex moral reasoning doesn't mean that he or she acts upon it. Indeed, some of the most frightening figures on the stage of life are the bright "character disorders" or "psychopathic deviates" who use moral reasoning to manipulate others (by way of their morality), much as a marionette master controls puppets. These psychologically sick persons are sometimes referred to as "moral morons." This is true in regard to their *behavior*: they are absolutely selfish and "childish" (in the worst sense of the word) in the motivation of their behavior. But bright psychopaths are geniuses in their ability to stand above the moral principles of their associates, to figure them out, and then to use that knowledge to their own advantage in controlling behavior.

Complexity: Characteristic #1 of Highest Intelligence[3]

A. Sam is stronger than George. George is weaker than Billy.

   Question: Who is the weakest?

   _____

B. All good musicians have a good sense of rhythm.
   Some persons with good rhythm can "carry a tune."
   None who have poor senses of rhythm are good dancers.
   All good dancers are well coordinated physically.
   Some good singers cannot read music, but all can carry a tune.

   Question: Can all good ballerinas read music?

   _____

Illustration A is one step into adult thought. The correct answer demands the ability to keep the interrelation of three, not just two, persons straight to make correct conclusions. Illustration B is much further advanced because it includes many and more complex interrelationships.

Objectivity: Characteristic #2 of Highest Intelligence

Objectivity is the ability to step out of (or rise above) your situation and see yourself and your associates from a detached vantage point. It is the difference between the actor in a play and the actor-director. If you are an actor you focus on *your* relationships in the play. You evaluate the other roles and players in relation to *your* role and how well they permit *you* to play it. However, if you are the actor-director, you must step out of your role and the way you are playing it and look at the total maze of roles and adjust them for the best artistic result. To be "subjective," that is, to consider only how the others play to you, would endanger the play as a whole, for the sake of one of its roles or players.

Abstraction: Characteristic #3 of Highest Intelligence

"Abstract" is sometimes used synonymously for "objective," carrying the meaning of being detached or objective in one's critical judgment. But its primary meaning is the ability to perceive the principle or essence of something. For instance, one abstraction most of us know is "catness." It is the *common* quality that all cats have whether they be Persian, alley, bearcat, tiger, etc. To accuse someone of being "catty" is applying this abstraction. Reconsider our illustration of the actor-director: what must you do to successfully *select* a play for production? To do that you must distill the essence or abstract the principle or theme in all the plays you read and critically evaluate them in light of your acting, stage, and financial resources as well as your audience. This demands detachment, analysis, and comfort with complexity. Playwrights take this process one step further. They can also create alternate ways of expressing these themes.

To illustrate how this relates to morality, contrast the average citizen in a socialist, capitalistic, or communistic state with a political theorist. Average citizens, with Level II Conventional morality, look from within their political systems and judge the other systems inferior. Why? Because of the political assumptions they've been taught and the power of propaganda. However, the Postconventional (Level III) theorist stands above these systems, abstracts the principles of politics, and raises questions about each of the systems and the survival of everyone in the militant clash of them. The theorist may give allegiance to the highest one or create a new system which might enable humankind to survive with dignity. The theorist might even suggest practical ways, in the complexity of our interrelated systems, to get there. How is that superior intelligence? It's objective (above it all), complex (able to conceptualize all interactions at once), and abstract (pushing on to higher principles of political order).

Level III: The World, the Universe, ALL

The threshold of Postconventional morality is this thought, "How strange it is that I and we should live in the country with the best political system and believing the one true religion." Moral reasoners step through the door and into Level III when they actually contrast their beliefs with others *as if they were equals*, in other words, "objectively."

This is sometimes called "the identity crisis." It's when a person, typically one in late adolescence, leaves the security of a set of personal commitments and rules, and critically evaluates their adequacy for his or her life. Now, this "moral relativism" can be very frightening to both youngster and parent. Sometimes other religions or ideologies are tried out. Other times it appears that a youngster regresses to Preconventional (selfish) morality, like the prodigal son who left "home" both physically and morally for a time. But, like the prodigal, when the son comes back from his excursion into the far country, his morality is no "secondhand" affair. He has stepped back from it, judged it, found it adequate, and committed himself to it.

This step was recorded by the ideological martyr Dag Hammarskjold. We would expect the U.N. leadership post to draw a person whose moral perspective was the world (and perhaps the universe, and the ALL). The stalwart Swede had to rise above national loyalty and attain objectivity, to abstract the issues dividing national interests and evaluate them in recognition of their complexities. He states about his personal pilgrimage:

> I now recognize and endorse unreservedly those very beliefs which were handed down to me. . . . When I finally reached that point, the beliefs in which I was once brought up and which, in fact had given my life direction even while my intellect still challenged their validity, were recognized by me as mine in their own right and by free choice. I feel that I can endorse those convictions without any compromise with the demands of that intellectual honesty which is the very key to maturity of mind.[4]

I once spoke to a bright young man who had always planned to be a minister (like his father and grandfather) but who pursued a graduate program in another academic area for two years, even teaching sections of it at the college level. He said that he did this because otherwise, when he was in the ministry and had doubts, he would always wonder how much he would have enjoyed this other field. One year of graduate school convinced him of his "social objectivity," and that he was called to be a minister. He could embrace it knowing that he was not just programmed, but had made an informed choice.

It was as if he, like Dag Hammarskjold, had stopped the world, gotten off, judged the commitments inculcated from family, church, and nation against the others available and perhaps by new ones, and then gotten back on the world in about the same place. However, the person before and after was not the same person.

Stage 5 Morality

Stage 5's technical name is "The social-contract, legalistic orientation." The "social contract" concept is the thesis that the rulers rule only with the permission of the ruled as opposed to the divine right of kings or some kind of dictatorship. As civilizations have developed, their ideas about freedom, self-development, and the quality of life have changed. For this reason the American social contract is set up for change through a legal, orderly process. This is what happens in the amendments to the Constitution—the community changes its social contract with itself.

Notice: the law is seen as a *means* of implementing something greater, and not an *end* in and of itself.

Let's say that America's citizens came to the conclusion that their present country was not the best way to "life, liberty, and the pursuit of happiness." Perhaps forming a United States of North America or of the Northern Hemisphere or of the Oil Consuming Nations would better accomplish this goal. The person whose mental and moral perspective is the world, the universe, and ALL, would have no qualms about changing the rules (the scope and even type of government) to achieve this end. However, it would be unthinkable for the person whose commitment was to his or her group and "system." After all, "It was good enough for George Washington and it's good enough for me."

Stage 5 Salvation:
Objective Commitment

We should expect bright, morally advanced Christians to have stepped back and made the faith their own. For them it will not be a secondhand faith simply absorbed, like a regional accent, from their environments. In that sense it is objective.

It should also be characterized by a commitment to Christ in using one's intelligence to abstract and respond to root problems in a very *complex* world. This leads to the controversial topic of the Christian's involvement in "social structures." Ernest T. Campbell outlines three levels of ministry performed by the church: (1) One-to-one acts of kindness, (2) Organized benevolence—by organizations such as the YMCA, welfare, or the church—to individuals, (3) Efforts "to change the structures that produce the hungry, the thirsty, the stranger, the naked, the sick, and the imprisoned."[5]

Campbell's illustration is the Christian response to the plight of the migrant laborers. At the first level the Christian might befriend a migrant or give candy to or play games with some migrant children. At the second level the Christian might work with the local churches to set up day care centers for the children, get the health authorities to provide services, procure voluntary legal aid, etc. But finally, at the third level, the Christian might see that he or she was just patching up the symptoms of persons who are being systematically hurt by an economic-political "structure" or setup.

Thus, the energies of the Christians who are convicted that they must root out the cause will be spent in solutions which deal with the basic problem. So, one Christian group may choose to support the inclusion of migrants in the minimum wage legislation. Others, such as Dr. Campbell, may elect to support the unionization of farm workers. The dedication of Dr. Campbell's excellent book, *Where Cross the Crowded Ways, Prayers of a City Pastor*, states

> This book is dedicated to the work and vision of Cesar Chavez, and all royalties have been assigned to the United Farm Worker's Union.[6]

That's putting your money where your mouth is.

Social Liberals and Conservatives

In *The Ten Largest Sunday Schools and What Makes Them Grow*, Elmer L. Towns observes that for people of his persuasion "personal salvation is primary: social action is secondary."[7] Dr. Jack Hyles, pastor of the church with "the fastest growing Sunday School" is quoted, "Our church does more social gospel work secondarily than most liberal churches do primarily."[8] However, an examination of the social programs of Dr. Hyles' and the other nine churches shows only the heal-the-symptom types of ministries (day care, hot lunch, etc.). This is Dr. Campbell's second level strategy and a concept of Conventional morality. Dr. Hyles had no plan to assault what "liberals" consider to be the root causes of these unfortunates' misfortunes. Campbell's third level demands the Postconventional perspective.

Postconventional Morality and the Nation-State

Social liberals assert that the prime cause of injustice at all levels is the political-economic system. The system of laws, the selective enforcement of laws, social pressures, etc. either evolved or was designed to give the few preferential treatment at the expense of the many. The largest, most dangerous system today, they contend, is the nation-state.

Lady Barbara Ward, in the "liberal" *Presbyterian Outlook*, affirms two principles of justice.[9] The first is "subsidiarity," the rule that larger bodies (counties, states, etc.) have no right to take responsibilities which can be better handled at the lower levels of government (towns, villages, etc.). Empire building from high places, such as when state bureaus try to take power away from counties and towns, is a familiar illustration of this sin. Conventional morality with its "State's rights" concerns can cope with this moral attack.

The second principle, "effective responsibility," requires a Postconventional mindset. It asserts that in some situations the common good is promoted by power being given by lower to higher levels of government. In addition to the obvious interstate concerns of health, transportation, radio and TV airwave rights, etc., even the State Na-

tional Guard may be nationalized if it is being used to infringe upon the rights of some citizens of that state.

If each nation-state, unwilling to surrender any of its powers or prerogatives, continues to press its national goals, then the whole world will suffer or be destroyed. Thus, people with this "liberal" perspective often raise their children to think of themselves primarily as world, not national, citizens. Their moral preoccupation is the nations' interdependence, not each country's independence. Likewise, in religious affairs, their principal loyalty is likely to be ecumenical, not denominational.

Ecumenical Concern and Church "Reunion"

Most Christians have little difficulty in accepting that the church is one in Christ Jesus. However, churches haven't been able visibly to express that unity well. These divisions confused Asian and African Christians and embarrassed and frustrated the missionaries who worked with them during the last century. So, the recent move toward ecumenical cooperation and toward church union was originally spearheaded by the missionary enterprise.[10]

Since the second World War there has appeared a strong movement toward church union. In the United States this is symbolized by the merger of some denominations and the Consultation on Church Union (COCU), a plan to unite about a dozen Protestant denominations. Protestant and Anglican visitors to Roman Catholic events and *vice versa* were part of the rising tide of ecumenism in the 1960s. The tide has waned in the 1970s, but the urgency to express oneness in Christ demanded the intellectual perspective of objectivity. It requires the willingness to get beyond "*my* group" (stage 3) and its ways of doing things—its (stage 4) laws and the orderly procedures related thereto— and cooperate with the world, the universe, and the ALL.

Stage 5 Salvation: Moral Relativism

Stage 5 moral thinking about salvation would involve all the perspectives discussed in the preceding. It would be objective: these Christians would have stepped back from their faith and critically compared it with other faith commitments before wholeheartedly re-embracing it. Because of this objective detour there will be less denominational fixation. Each Christian group is seen as the response of Christians within a historical situation. Each is a kind of "historical accident." One next logical step would be a concern to transcend history and fulfill the oneness reflected in Christ's prayer for the church through denominational re-unions. This transcendence is called "ecumenism." Social rather than personal ethics is another logical step. The program agenda for the church is social action because that gets at the roots of problems which are, by definition, "complex."

Christians at stage 5 would be less sure of the perfection of their belief system and moral adequacy. Where the stage 4 law and order Christians must distort the ethical problem to fit one of the rules (if it doesn't fit), stage 5 Christians will alter a rule or rules when confronted by an ethical dilemma that is impolite enough not to fit their rule system. This different strategy was what so enraged many Christians when Joseph Fletcher's *Situation Ethics* (Westminster, 1966) was published. Fletcher argued that stage 4, law and order, "moralistic" ethics were inadequate to cope with certain current ethical issues. To force ethical problems to fit the old rules won't work. When two rules conflict, such as when the patriotic spy is asked to sacrifice sexual purity for country, we must get our bearings from the ultimate rule, Christian love.[11]

Most of the debate boiled down to the difference between the mindsets of the stage 4 and 5 persons. The 4s were not willing to permit themselves or their loved ones to be cast into the stage 5 sea of moral relativism. In other words, a world without hard-and-fast rules was incomprehensible. This is the attractiveness of Bill Gothard's Institute: it intends to give Christians a divinely inspired system which will provide the solution to any problem. It will be a wall around them, keeping them from ever having to get out into that sea of moral relativism. Jeb Magruder's excuse of "situation ethics" as justification for some of the illegal and unethical activities exposed in Watergate brought forth an "I told you so!" from this wing of the church. The far left responded that the analysis oversimplified the problem. A seminary professor said, "Our problem now is a general belieflessness, a nonideological commitment to the system."[12]

Do evil people corrupt good systems or do evil systems corrupt good people? Stage 4 affirms the former and stage 5 the latter. From the perspective of either, there is no way the other can be right.

"Jesus Christ Frees and Unites"

The World Council of Churches would have to say that its concern is for persons within systems. Though its answer to the above question would be "both," it is more identified with working *through systems*. This stage 5 perspective is clearly enunciated in this quotation from a preparatory report for the fifth Assembly meeting on the theme "Jesus Christ Frees and Unites."

Jesus Christ frees—whom? All human beings—indeed all creation—from the slavery of sin. If we accept him as Lord and Savior, we also accept the call to make his liberation known by sharing in the struggles of men and women to achieve liberation from all that oppresses in this world.

Christ's freedom cannot be divided up. None of us can be fully free while others are suffering. How then can we best share in the struggle for liberation?

There are at least four ways. First, the effects of injustice can be alleviated through social service and help to individuals or groups. Second, through concerted action, especially in economic planning, the earth's resources can be more evenly distributed. Third, there is direct political struggle to do away with the basic causes of injustice. Fourth, social education, sometimes called conscientization, can make people aware of their own potential and lead them to take charge of their own affairs. Each of these ways needs the others. No one of these is "more Christian" than the others. Judging which is most appropriate depends on a careful examination of the specific factors of each particular situation.[13]

The *World*, the Universe, ALL

To sum up, the world is the perspective of the stage 5 Christian. Whereas Conventional Christians can take a "my country, right or wrong" type of view because their group defines what is right and wrong, Postconventional believers must evaluate their country and their religion as simply one among equals. The "good news" is this: because they can understand the complexity of the world and abstract the underlying principles of various political and religious appeals, their commitment is one which has been tried and found adequate. The Conventional Christians have never "tested" their faith. The "bad news" is this: they lack the unquestioned assurance of the Conventional Christians and they possess a social ethics viewpoint which is both threatening and possibly incomprehensible to their Conventional friends.

Stage 6: Universal Ethical Principle

Right is defined by the decision of conscience in accord with self-chosen *ethical principles* appealing to logical comprehensiveness, universality, and consistency. These principles are abstract and ethical (the Golden Rule, the categorical imperative); they are not concrete moral rules like the Ten Commandments. At heart, these are universal principles of *justice*, of the *reciprocity* and *equality* of the human *rights*, and of respect for the dignity of human beings as *individual persons*.[14]

If every government, every citizen of every country, every religion believed that it was right to let die at birth persons who would be classified as severely retarded, would that make it right? Stage 6 clearly might say *no* because of its concern for the sacredness of life. It affirms that there are some values or truths which are self-evident, which no majority has any right to deny. Its Christians join with God in building a world in which *all systems* support these rights. The rights are *ends*, the systems are merely the *means*. The opposite is true in stage 4.

A Christian of stage 6 has a deep awareness of the transcendent. The focus moves beyond the world, to the *universe and ALL*. James Fowler describes it:

> At stage six one's selfhood and position, *vis-à-vis* the transcendent, are "known" or experienced simultaneously as ultimately relative and relatively ultimate. There is identification in or with the ultimate which transforms previous integratedness and faith. The symbols, traditions and relations of determinate community are still seen as mediative of the ultimate. At the same time all determinate communities are unified in a cosmic common-wealth of being, inclusive of all power and value. [15]

Because of their superior intelligence and transcendent perspective, stage 6 Christians can perceive a meaning that is hidden from their Conventional counterparts. "The world's organizations prove that evil rules the world till Christ rings down the curtain of history and God ascends the judgment throne," says the Conventional Christian. "Not so," comes the Postconventional response. "God is working in this apparent chaos to bring the world to fulfillment in himself."

Teilhard de Chardin exemplified this perspective. In 1915 this Catholic soldier-priest was given a medal for his "contempt for danger" as a stretcher-bearer. The gifted thinker wrote after carrying the mangled dead and alive from the battlefield:

> "Through the present war we have really progressed in civilization. To each phase of the world's development there corresponds a certain new profoundness of evil . . . which integrates with the growing free energy for good." [16]

What did he see in war that the other stretcher-bearers missed? He saw the war as a means through which Christ was bringing about the redemptive unification of the world.

For Conventional Christians the positive thing about salvation is that it redeems relationships with other people. Postconventional Christians go further: they see Christ working through groups, groups of groups, institutions of law, mercy, etc., and, in all humanity's complex interactions! Philip Potter of the World Council of Churches says that:

> "salvation in Christ . . . is concerned with the liberation of persons and societies from all that prevents them from living an authentic existence in justice and shared community . . . the church itself needs to be saved, liber-

ated from all that is false to the revolutionary, convicting, and renewing nature of the Gospel." [The church itself needs to be saved because of its] "racial, economic, and cultural captivity."[17]

We might continue, à la Teilhard's biological model, that Christians share in this onward (evolutionary) and upward (atoning) activity of God.

Conflict Between Levels

Enough has been said to show that a clash of opinions is almost inevitable between Christians of the Conventional and Postconventional viewpoints. The former with inerrant Bible in hand busily dot the i's and cross the t's of fixed systematic theology which places the legal view of salvation at its center. Such Christians scrupulously apply this change-less faith to every personal relationship they are involved in. If a life situation does not fit their faith system, they will alter the situation rather than change the system.[18] Legalists could not participate in the Underground Railroad during the Civil War because it was illegal, whereas Postconventional moralists simply appealed to a higher law and took the risk. The Postconventionals' system was more complex because it made room for exceptions to the general rule. A strict stage 4 legalist would have a hard time being a spy in our intelligence program, whereas stage 3 (my country, right or wrong) or stage 5 or 6 persons (both of whom hold to "higher laws" or exceptions to normal rules of behavior) could do it in good conscience, but for different moral reasons. Both groups— Conventional and Postconventional—respect the same rules; but Post-conventionals sometimes deviate, not because they want to break the rules, but because for them the rules are not ends but means. They are marching to the beat of a "different" drummer.

Process Theology

Perhaps the root of the conflict between Conventionals and Postcon-ventionals is in the differing philosophical assumptions. Robert Mellert, in his book *What Is Process Theology?*, points out that most of us have inherited a static view of the universe from the Greek philosopher Parmenides. "Law" and "being" are topics which assume that you can deal with them as essences. Heraclitus's concept of reality was the oppo-site. "No one ever steps into the same river twice" is the observation we associate with him. He meant that the underlying quality of reality was change, not constancy, becoming not being.[19] Change and becoming are things more consistent with Teilhard's view of evolutionary development toward Christ. The *process* and its direction would be the ultimate loyalty. That most conventional folk would find difficult to understand.

Humanism, Pantheism, and Universalism

Conventional Christians consider their Postconventional colleagues to be courting all three of these heresies. Protagorus defined humanism for most people with his dictum: "Man is the measure of all things." Postconventional Christians are accused of doing that when they elevate *their understanding* of the Christ of the Scripture above some systematic understanding or confession of faith or the Scriptures themselves. William R. Jones asserts that we have no choice. Abraham's act of preparing to sacrifice Isaac illustrates this point.[20] Abraham had to decide if it was God or Moloch who was commanding him to kill his son. He would obey God, not Moloch, but *he* had to decide in this very exceptional situation. From the Conventional religious perspective, Postconventional Christians appear to be putting themselves in the judgment seat rather than simply trying to obey God's system of laws and rules which everyone (in our group) agrees upon.

Pantheism sees the laws and forces in the universe or all-that-is as the Divine. This is the opposite of the Christian view which radically separates the Creator from his creation, the doctrine of the "transcendence" of God. When God is seen in-the-process-of, or "immanent" in, the creation, as Teilhard's evolution toward the Omega conceives of him, it is just one step to stating that God *is* the universe-in-meaningful-process.

Universalism is the belief that all persons will be saved. As some see it, Christ willed it, died for it, and it's a *fait accompli*. Evangelism is enabling people to see what already is.[21] Thus, God is not to be frustrated. Human history is headed into oneness in Christ and people may join in with the process or fight it, but the end result is sure.

The Classic View of the Atonement

In *Christus Victor*, Gustaf Aulen (New York: Macmillan, 1931) argues that the classic view of salvation, more evident in the Lutheran and Catholic traditions, is a "safeguard." This saves us from the limitations of the legal view of salvation by replacing the Biblical illustration of the lawcourt with the Biblical figure of Christ the leader of the Christian soldiers who move onward. All of history since the decisive battle with evil, which was won at the cross and tomb, is movement toward the final, perfect, and complete victory. Everything and everyone will be possessed by Christ.

The military model of how God is saving the world makes Teilhard's views less of a threat. The evolution of a war and of a cosmos are highly similar. Christians are participating, as soldiers, in the salvation of the world. They do this with every effort to "humanize" life, that is, make it like the perfect life lived by Jesus of Nazareth. The kind of humanism which Luther referred to when using the phrase "the deification of human nature" can be applied to individuals, groups, systems, institutions, etc., which are moving toward the Omega point, because Christ's victory is sure.

Pantheism loses some of its bite because in the military model territory as well as persons are claimed. The pantheistic and universalistic strains in the Christian tradition agree that everything and everyone will be claimed and perfected by the conquering son.

Part ▮▮▮

20/20 Corrected

6 Youth Evangelism: Its Power Is Its Peril

Our virtues are most frequently but vices in disguise.
La Rochefoucauld, *Maxims*

Rather, speaking the truth in love, we are to grow up in every way into him who is the head, into Christ.
Eph. 4:15

The 1974 General Assembly of the Presbyterian Church, U.S. adopted as a strategy for the following year to "evaluate the theologies and techniques of non-church, Christian youth movements."[1] This reflects an ambivalence toward these groups which all have a concept of and a concern for evangelism. Should a local church become a sponsor of a youth club? Should wage earners give part of their tithe to such movements? Should parents encourage their youngsters to get involved? How should local church youth programs respond to these groups that appear to attract and repulse people? These are gut questions that people ask. The answers are complex! Moral stage theory may help them to understand the whole issue better.

Wall or Foundation?

One way to afford a house is to live in its cellar while you save your rent money to make a down payment on the mortgage to build the rest. This means living in a cement block building, the top half of which sticks out of the ground, with a tar paper flat roof and a small chimney stuck out the side. Now there are two ways for people in this situation to look at their homes: as walls or as a foundation. It's a wall when you see yourself stuck at or satisfied with this level of building. You could spend your whole life in this "house" and be adequately sheltered. In fact, the dramatic increase in the cost of housing makes some aspire to no higher building. The walls, then, are limits, the end of the building's development.

On the other hand those cement blocks may be seen as a foundation: one which provides adequate but *temporary* shelter because there is further building to do. And so you do not fix up the basement too much, but save the time and expense for the home above. These are two different mindsets and they do affect behavior.

This is analogous to our view of evangelistic youth movements: do they present themselves to youth as walls which enclose everything you need to live the rest of your life, or as a solid foundation on which God builds (or grows) the mature creation (Col. 2:7)?

When a "House" Shouldn't Become a Home

Each stage in moral development is a place where you feel "at home." It does not deny one's previous home, but builds on it. The problem here is that most youths *and* adults are at stage 3 and 4 moral levels. Since these levels represent such a majority, a "great silent majority" some call it, there is a tendency for stage 4 people to think that they have arrived at their ultimate destination in moral and religious development. This is especially true of older adolescents. Some have arrived, we must admit, but others have the potential to go on.

The systematic nature of stage 4 also gives its population this "having arrived" feeling. For the *first time* in these people's lives religious moral views form an organized whole. And, having just arrived there, it's hard to think of going beyond the system. Thus, for Conventionals, anything that smacks of "situational" or "contextual" ethics is, by definition, wrong. These Christians shun anti-legal ethics. They are "worldly." But for others, contextual ethics may just be another name for stage 5 or 6 moral thinking. The simplicity and comprehensiveness of stage 4 is also the problem which makes the legal or "substitutionary" doctrine of the atonement the *only* way to think of this divine act—it rules out the dimensions of the atonement which the other doctrines and their supporting Biblical material can give the Christian.

Yes and No

I believe that much of the negative criticism of independent Christian youth movements is misplaced or unfounded because, in essence, it is a criticism of stage 3 and 4 morality from a stage 5 or 6 perspective. It is precisely the moral clarity and focus of these Conventional groups which connects with the way the vast majority of kids think. "Good" evangelism should meet people where they are *but also* encourage their growth in the faith. This, I believe, is the moral stage contribution to the youth evangelism controversy: *the precision of the Conventional moral stage focus is both a strength and a weakness.*

To flesh out this position, I would like to analyze some typical criticisms of various non-denominational youth movements. The criticisms analyzed are those to which moral stage theory can give insight.

Criticism #1: They Are Simplistic

Non-denominational and inter-denominational youth groups are stuck with lowest common denominators. To get involved in such doctrinal issues as the sacraments would cut off their broad base of support. To take positions on complex (stage 5) social questions would also offend blocks of backers.

The American Sunday School movement faced this same problem before the Civil War. It had to avoid virtually all of the doctrinal issues dividing most of the denominations because it was their chief educational program. Thus, it stuck with the "simple" gospel. "Simplification" meant not only limiting the gospel doctrinally, but steering it clear of social concerns. For instance, the Sunday School dealt with the complex question of slavery by ignoring it. When it did mention slavery, terms like "that peculiar institution" were used. The Nat Turner rebellion complicated the posture of the Sunday School Union because it was discovered that Nat learned to read (and think) in a Sunday School. So, in the South, Sunday Schools for slaves were suppressed. Where white missionaries were allowed to run Sunday Schools for blacks they emphasized they would teach their pupils, as the Apostle did, "to be obedient unto their own masters, and to please them well in all things." The reaction of the British Sunday School to this sellout was disgust. The Americans damned only alcohol, while the British damned war and slavery in addition.[2]

The British Sunday School had faced the same basic problem about a century earlier. The English power structure had argued that teaching the poor to read would cause them to become dissatisfied and cause trouble (especially if those factory "hands" read about a French stage 5 concept, the social contract). The leaders of the Sunday School replied that one of their basic goals was "to bring men cheerfully to submit to their stations."[3]

The gospel can no longer be considered "simple" when it is thought of in stage 5 terms, because that is the level where its social implications come center stage. It is also the stage at which most people aren't, and might be thought of as the point of financial fallout (in terms of support). Thus, youth evangelism organizations have a natural advantage over socially conscious denominations. By gearing their message to the moral levels of most youth with either a simple integration of faith or a not too complex set of spiritual principles, they scratch where the kids itch and do not threaten their backers.

But what will happen to those young Christians if these simply integrated principles are presented as dogma? If the youths pass into adulthood never going beyond stage 4 thinking, they will become backers of the movement, probably. However, if their thought processes mature *and* they apply stage 5 thinking to their faith, they will have to (1) suppress this new view, (2) discard their faith, or (3) reintegrate their religious thinking at the next higher stage. Youth organizations which prepare youngsters for option 3 have a disadvantage when it comes to precision and support but an advantage when it comes to preparing youngsters for more complex moral judgments.

Criticism #2: They Have Inadequate Doctrines of the Church and Salvation

David Ng concludes his criticism of Campus Crusade's view of the church by stating that, "Evangelism is more than a personal conversion; it is the developing of a person-who-is-a-part-of-a-community in a dynamic context of varied relationships and experiences,"[4] a congregation. This is a classic stage 5 concept of the church and salvation, and a stage 5 criticism of the "Conventional" view of these same doctrines. Stage 3's "my small group and Jesus" and stage 4's "our group's simple integration of faith which guarantees us salvation" cannot cope with the complexities of persons in communities and systems within systems (political, economic, etc.).

In defense of Conventional "teen" morality, it's very hard for most youngsters to think of themselves as members of the total maze of relationships in a local and larger congregation. Their perspective is the relationships within their circle of friends and family and to their country. "I am Pat, of the Smiths of Smalltown, part of U.S.A. and the United Methodist Church." They can easily identify with a smaller group, such as an independent (or even congregational) youth group and with a system of beliefs which is simple enough to understand and is valued by the group with which they identify. This is where their cognitive equipment functions efficiently.

The real ox-goring done by many independent youth groups, according to many local churches, is that they decide which churches are true or "Bible-believing" ones. The youngsters are exhorted to attend these. This, too, is stage 3 and 4 simplicity. "Our group has the truth; ergo, others do not have the truth." At stage 5 a person is able to stand outside his or her religious group, as well as others, and see the possibility of error and truth in any and all of them. At stage 5 one wonders, "How unlikely that I was brought up in what appears to be the one true religion in the world!"

Dean Kelley in his book, *Why Conservative Churches Are Growing*, asserts that strictness is one trait of the growing church. By "strictness" he means:

1. Absolutism—we have the only, complete, unambiguous explanation of the truth;
2. Conformity—members who think differently must confess their errors or be shunned;
3. Fanaticism—we'll share our truth but since it is the only truth we won't seriously engage in dialogue.[5]

This is an excellent description of stage 4, "walled in" religious commitment. It has the driving force of meaning to believers in their faith and practice. "Practice" here means the enforcement of belief, life-style, and out-going (not dialogue-type) witness. It appeals to the moral stage mindset of the majority of adults and teens who think at the Conventional Level. A "Biblical" church is one that thinks and therefore acts as we do. And these "conservative" churches are the ones who are giving money, adding missionaries, building churches, and increasing their Sunday School enrollments.

When Dean Kelley analyzes this question of the church's view of itself, he concludes that the deciding factor in whether a religious group should consider a social expression of the gospel as its responsibility is, "How will this activity help make clearer the ultimate meaning of life to our members?" If the position can be fitted into the members' understanding of what the church is supposed to be and do then, Kelley says, go and sell it. If not, he says that the activity will seem secondary to the members and will erode the unity and force of the group.[6]

Kelley's is a pragmatic, organization theory explanation of this issue. Moral stage theory is another approach. Taking a stand *against* pornography is a simple position: filth debauches our youth, etc. Taking a stand for total freedom of expression is far more complex: when the press isn't free, the government, pressure groups, etc. curtail the freedom of thought and dissent. The former is stage 4 (thou shalt not think or purvey pornography; neither thou nor anyone who is in the city limits). The latter is stage 5 (freedom of expression in tension with the moral values of the community). Being against alcohol can be simple (your body is God's temple and don't get drunk) while withdrawing investments against a nation which practices racism is more complex. Kelley asserts that the mainline churches have not failed because they've taken social positions, but because they haven't educated their memberships "up" to the more complex social implications of the gospel.

As with the doctrine of the church, so too the stage 4 legal view of salvation can become a wall restricting growth, or a foundation on which to build. The mindset which is most comfortable with the legal imagery of the atonement tends to simplify ethical problems to fit its rules of behavior. This seems to be most vividly portrayed in the Basic Youth Conflicts Seminars—Gothard's followers consider his system an umbrella of protection from moral impurity. But what if the moral issue is so complex that the system can't handle it? Smuggling Bibles into Communist countries places law violations against the Great Commission. Who says which commitment takes precedence? Should a raped, pregnant, single woman be permitted to have an abortion? Here the welfare of one individual is pitted against another! The options are (a) to simplify the situations so that one religious rule will appear right while all other options are wrong, or (b) to think "contextually," meaning in a stage 5 fashion. To do "situational" thinking demands the mental ability to do the most complex form of moral theology. Not many people, including adolescents, can do that.

In conclusion, the legal view of salvation, which is the most systematic one, appears to fit the moral stage of most youths. It tends to be the basis of a moralistic code of ethics. Youth movements that study and prize all Biblical views of the atonement can facilitate members (who are able intellectually) to develop a more complex view of salvation and of the ethical decision process. I believe that the image of salvation most compatible with stage 5 moral thinking is *Christ the Victor* or leader of the church which is to fight evil in every form and place on earth.

Criticism #3: They Have a Subjective Rather Than an Objective Concept of Salvation

Sociologist Rodney Stark found that middle- and upper-class English church members tended to "do" their religion. The lower classes, however, tended to "feel" or "believe" theirs.[7] It may be that the progression in levels of religious orientation, feeling-believing-doing, are the normal expressions of the three moral stage Levels. Preconventional persons are very subjective: they fear the consequences of hell and desire the bliss of heaven. In short, their religious direction is what feels or will feel good. God punishes these people with anxiety when they are wrong and rewards them with a glow when they've done right. Conventional persons internalize values: they share a belief system with their group and find their behavior controlled by their group. They are more objective and intellectual than Preconventionals in that they give loyalty to a belief system. Finally, Postconventionals transcend these other Levels by giving loyalty to a system of beliefs which they have stood apart from and judged convicting. They apply *it* in their behavior to the total world of decisions: personal ones as well as those with complex ethical interrelations. Note, their "doing" is not dictated by loyalty to a group *per se.* Though they may be members of a church, they are directed by inner selected ethics. They are the most objective because they are the least dependent upon group approval. Their devotion is to the ultimate reality: God.

Each of these components of faith can and does criticize the other's weakness. The charismatic and Jesus movements ask the systematizers and ethics calculators, "Where is your joy?" Campus Crusade, however, instructs its members not to trust feeling. "Feeling" is like the caboose, while "Fact" is the engine and "Faith" is the tender. Bill Bright teaches in *Have You Made the Wonderful Discovery of the Spirit-Filled Life?* that Christians should be objective, banking on the fact of redemption and their faith in it, not the feeling reactions of commitment.[8]

Samuel S. Hill gives a dramatic illustration of Postconventional's "doing" criticism of Conventional's "believing." During the 1960s, at a high-level denominational meeting, a socially liberal editor was arguing that integration was integral to the gospel. A middle-of-the-road Southern pastor took the wind out of his sails by pointing out that ethical responsibility in race was not a "part of the plan of salvation" and that it was not right to make it so.[9] Postconventional's critique of Conventional's belief is that the "plan" or system of doctrine one must believe is so walled in that it cannot be a foundation for what the Christian ought to do in race relations.

Criticism #4: They Use Hero Worship

Virtually all the youth movements use young leaders, usually recent college or seminary graduates who have received special training in youth evangelism. Young Life is unabashedly leader-centered.[10] The Fellowship of Christian Athletes and Athletes in Action (just like the old Youth for Christ "Devil's Saturday Night" rallies) use the celebrity witness as one *modus operandi.* Though Inter-Varsity and Youth for Christ emphasize leaders as coaches, group process guides, etc., they are well aware of the influence of their leaders among the impressionable adolescents to whom they minister.

Why are these older adolescent leaders so influential? Objectively speaking, we could observe that most of them are attractive, personable, bright, and skilled practitioners, who do this work at a real financial sacrifice to themselves. Subjectively speaking, we could add that it seems to be some combination of their sensitivity to God's presence and leading, empathy with kids, deep concern, and, possibly, charisma.

Of course, though, since many of the youth with whom they work are at, or one stage beyond, Christ(ian)-the-model, leader attractiveness is a "natural" factor in their ability to influence young people. And it's questionable whether *any* large movement—adolescent or adult—can get along without its heroes. It's easier to localize one's loyalty in a president than a congress, a virtuoso than an orchestra, a star than a team, Jesus than the Trinity, a college than a consortium, an executive than a committee, and so on. Thus, to believe that people in general, let alone adolescents in particular, won't be influenced by heroes of one sort or other ignores the nature of people. The real question is, "To what kind of models will we expose our youth?" Perhaps the genius of the Peace Corps, VISTA, the Mormon missionary program, and other religious movements is precisely this use of older adolescents in work with younger ones. This process kills two birds with one stone: it harnesses the idealism of some of the most committed older adolescents and uses that to positively influence the younger adolescents.

Manipulation—the Unresolved Issue

Moral stage theory asserts that influence by identification is inevitable. But tied in with this criticism are others. *Christian Century* editor J. Claude Evans reasons that one factor in the "theological shallowness" (stage 4 morality) of Campus Crusade is Bill Bright's decision *not* to hire seminary graduates. "Non-seminary-trained personnel are less apt to ask probing theological questions and to muddy the waters of a clear-flowing evangelistic stream," he says.[11] For "probing questions" we might substitute "stage 5, structural morality questions." Seminary students often move to stage 5 moral thinking. Their commitment to a system of doctrine and ethics is less cocky than stage 4 college graduates who have freshly discovered "the" system of truth. Further, stage 5 folks love to confront stage 4 folks with ethical situations which highlight the inadequacy of any closed system of beliefs. This causes the turmoil variously known as the "religious identity crisis" or "being awash in the sea of moral relativism." It definitely will not motivate financial backers of the Conventional moral persuasion to support the cause. Evans's implication is that by limiting leadership to Conventional morality's outlook Campus Crusade will make a strong impact on the college youth and avoid any "problems" related to more complex issues.

There have been other charges of manipulation. Youth for Christ's large rallies were considered by some as having the mass-psychology power over kids. The same criticism has been leveled at all large meetings: Inter-Varsity's Urbana Missionary meetings, Campus Crusade's Explo, Billy Graham's Crusades. Young Life is judged to be manipulative for using its "cultivate the chiefs to get the Indians" strategy. Campus Crusade's use of a survey form (which is not used for research as is implied) to get in an evangelistic witness is considered unethical. Etc.

All of the above charges of manipulation and many more can be and often are argued, for and against. I do not choose to discuss them, even though they are usually connected with the hero or model influence, because they do not relate to the moral stage issue.

7 Gospel Illustrations: What's Memorable May Be Irrelevant

"Christ is the answer!"
"Really? What's the question?"

When St. Paul got a hearing before the most intellectual audience of his career, he began his presentation of the Christian faith this way: " 'Men of Athens, I perceive that in every way you are very religious.' " (Acts 17:22, RSV) Now that was very clever because the word translated "religious" (in Greek, *deisidaimonesteros*) also means "superstitious," and is so translated in the King James Version. Since one person's religion is another's superstition, Paul managed to lick 'em without joining them and make them feel good at the same time. He got their attention, too!

After this opening line, the apostle continued by calling their attention to one of their numerous idols, the one "To an unknown god." This void in their pantheon could now be filled by the one true God who created everything, who made humanity of "one" ("one blood," KJV), and desired to unite all things in himself. The apostle quoted *their* poets to illustrate his point that we are God's "offspring" and all exist in him. Finally, he told them that the time of fulfillment had arrived because the now-revealed-to-them God had acted in the life, death, and resurrection of Jesus Christ.

Paul's speech did not move the masses that day. There was a handful of converts but the majority, who loved to hear the latest, elected to hear him later.

The preacher, teacher, and especially the evangelist share Paul's double challenge: establishing rapport with the hearers and aiming the gospel at their moral Level. It is noteworthy that Paul chooses to present the Christian faith as it is conceptualized at the Postconventional moral Level to these philosophers. He does not threaten them with hell, though he does speak of judgment; he does not assert that "our" faith is better just because it is ours (he bends over backwards to do the opposite) nor does he hammer with legal imagery; instead, he flirts with Stoic pantheism by conceptualizing humanity as part of the Oneness from which it came before Eden. In a word, Paul chooses the conceptualization of the gospel which fits the moral thought categories of his audience. There are elements of the other two moral Levels, but those could be understood by almost any audience. For these philosophical types, the most relevant understanding of a faith would have to be focused at the highest moral Level: the Postconventional.

Autopsy of a Disaster

Athens was Paul's major failure. Some critics suggest that Paul's assertion in 1 Corinthians 2:1, where he rejects "lofty words or wisdom," proves that Paul never did argue as it is recorded in Acts 17.[1] Others say that after the Areopagus disaster, Paul was convinced that philosophical argument would never achieve much for the gospel.[2] From a psycho-historical perspective, this rejection may have been traumatic to the apostle. When hearers either embrace the gospel or get so angry about it (or you) that they attempt to persecute, eliminate, or quiet you, you know that you are being taken seriously. But to be told, "That's very interesting, let's hear from you another day. (Don't call us, we'll call you.)" is devastating. From what we know about Paul's psyche it may have been responsible for his rejection of evangelism at the Postconventional Level. This may leave the reader with the impression that the "simple gospel" is safe but that complex, philosophical understandings of the gospel are dangerous. It might even be taken to baptize anti-intellectualism (see esp. 1 Cor. 1:18-29)!

If one ignores the history of the Christian church and sticks to the Bible, it would *appear* that the gospel should only be presented in its simpler forms, with reliance on the Holy Spirit for its effect. However, after Christianity got a beachhead among the poor and middle classes in the post-New Testament era, it was forced to do what Paul failed to accomplish at Athens: to present Christ intellectually and effectively to the learned and sophisticated. The tangible monument to this effort was the institution called the Catechetical School, which began as a University satellite at Alexandria, Egypt. The institution spread to Antioch, Edessa, and Nisbis, all centers of higher learning. The church fathers Clement and Origen produced their "formulation of theoretical and systematic theology" and other works which spoke to generations of intellectuals.[3] Relying on the Holy Spirit, they presented Christ at the higher moral Levels to bright Christians and all the educated who would listen.

My contention is that whether or not everyone knows it, the church has been preaching the gospel, *conceptualized at all the moral Levels* of the hearers, ever since the time of Jesus and the apostles. And, since good teachers, preachers, and debaters must illustrate their understanding of the faith at the various moral Levels, as Paul did when he quoted the pagan poets, I contend that the illustrations of salvation are good clues to the moral Level at which the gospel presenter is aiming.

Back to You

Let's pretend that you have been invited to speak to a group that you know nothing about, except that its members are "very much like you." Your topic is: "How I Think of Salvation." Five to ten minutes is your time allotment. You are told that that's enough time to give a Scripture citation, one good illustration, and a couple of very personal reflections to tie it all up. You accept this advice and turn to a book of illustrations to begin your preparation. (You tried reading all the references to salvation in the Bible but got overwhelmed, so you decided to come at it again via the illustration route.) The following are the only illustrations available to you (making up your own isn't fair for the purpose of what we're doing, so don't fudge!). Which one would you choose, and why?

A. Christ Brought Me Out

During my college days, I visited the county jail once a week with a Christian group. It was a worthwhile experience, but some of the prisoners seemed to resent our visits. One of them told us, "You can't tell me anything—your life's been too sheltered."

I did not know what to say, but a young man of our group started rolling up his sleeve. He pointed as he said, "See those scars? You know they were caused by heroin, don't you? That's why I don't think you can enlighten me too much about the seamy side of life. But Christ brought me out of that."

Here was one who had come through an addiction which could have crippled him for life. Yet he had met the One who transformed a dead life into a living, worthwhile one.[4]

B. The Only Way to Go

Transportation companies strive to make their mode of travel appear "the only way to go." Since all of us will have to make that great journey called death, maybe we should advertize by comparing the statements of the dying who chose to go with Christ with those who chose to go it alone. Dwight L. Moody, the evangelist, said, "This is glorious! Earth recedes; Heaven is opening; God is calling me!" But Voltaire, the French skeptic wailed, "I am abandoned by God and man; I shall go to hell!" The martyr, John Noise said, "Blessed be the time that ever I was born for this day," but the anguished Sir Francis Newport moaned, "Oh, that I could lie for a thousand years upon the fire that is never quenched, to purchase the favor of God and be united with Him again. But it is a fruitless wish. Millions and millions of years will bring me no nearer the end of my torments than one poor hour! Oh, the unsufferable pangs of Hell!"

C. The Call from Beyond

Blowing through heaven and earth, and in our hearts and the heart of every living thing, is a gigantic breath—a great Cry—which we call God. Plant life wished to continue its motionless sleep next to stagnant waters, but the Cry leaped up within it and violently shook its roots: "Away, let go of the earth, walk!" Had the tree been able to think and judge, it would have cried, "I don't want to. What are you urging me to do! You are demanding the impossible!" But the Cry, without pity, kept shaking its roots and shouting, "Away, let go of the earth, walk!"

It shouted in this way for thousands of eons; and lo! as a result of desire and struggle, life escaped the motionless tree and was liberated.

Animals appeared—worms—making themselves at home in water and mud. "We're just fine here," they said. "We have peace and security; we're not budging!"

But the terrible Cry hammered itself pitilessly into their loins. "Leave the mud, stand up, give birth to your betters!"

"We don't want to! We can't!"

"You can't, but I can. Stand up!"

And lo! after thousands of eons, man emerged, trembling on his still unsolid legs.

The human being is a centaur; his equine hoofs are planted in the ground, but his body from breast to head is worked on and tormented by the merciless Cry. He has been fighting, again for thousands of eons, to draw himself, like a sword, out of his animalistic scabbard. He is also fighting—this is his new struggle—to draw himself out of his human scabbard. Man calls in despair. "Where can I go? I have reached the pinnacle, beyond is the abyss." And the Cry answers, "I am beyond. Stand up!" All things are centaurs. If this were not the case, the world would rot into inertness and sterility.[5]

D. Justice and Love

There was the ancient and just ruler Zaleucis, king of the Locrians. One of his laws carried the penalty of blinding. Before the king was brought his own son proven guilty of the breaking of this stern law. What would the king do? Would he evade the claims of justice because he loved his son? He solved his problem by commanding that one of his son's eyes be put out and one of his own eyes. Two eyes were exacted for the crime. The king's justice was acclaimed. The king's love was marveled at.[6]

E. She Wouldn't Let Me!

Some years ago a well-known actress was hospitalized with appendicitis. She was in pain and the doctor strongly recommended surgery. However, she was very vain and was more concerned about the small scar which would be on her abdomen. She refused to sign the consent papers.

The physician ordered ice packs and other measures to forestall what could be the fatal consequences of her decision. He visited her again and again trying to show her that all she had to do to save her life was consent. She died before he convinced her.

F. The Scope of Salvation

"There are two great entities in human life, the human soul and the human race, and religion is to save both."[7]

The Low-Level Illustrations

Hellfire-and-damnation or punishment-and-reward illustrations are often considered too base a motivation to offer for the acceptance of the Christian faith. Nevertheless, just as Jonathan Edwards used the former in "Sinners in the Hands of an Angry God," so it is still found if you know where to stop, look, or listen. The tent meetings and revivals still have it, as does the evangelical wing of the church, especially in lower socio-economic groups. "The Only Way to Go" (Preconventional Level, stage 1) is a classic type of illustration because it trains our attention upon one's spiritual condition at the moment of death. Others of this kind tell about people who were "almost" persuaded but either weren't fully convinced or, because of some accident or circumstance, didn't know they were going to die in time to be persuaded. Like the rich farmer in Jesus' parable, they go off to sleep content because they have achieved the good life but are not prepared for the good death.

The most repugnant exploitation of this moral Level was found in the Middle Ages when those who believed that baptism erased "original" and all other sin from their souls took the grand risk. They chose to live without being baptized (if their parents had so neglected them), realizing that they risked hell if they died unforgiven. Their strategy was to "raise hell" all their lives and, when they believed that they were dying, get baptized, and thus have virtually all the punishment due them in hell or purgatory written off by this great timing. Like foxhole conversions and all others based on fear, one wonders at their validity. It seems to be a very immature or childish stance, perhaps valid only for those who are truly moral children.

The higher stage of this lowest moral Level emphasizes that we must cooperate or be willing to do something in order to achieve a reward or escape a punishment in the present or future. "She Wouldn't Let Me!" is typical of this medical group of illustrations which assert, "You will die if you do not accept this medicine, treatment, or surgery" (which may involve some inconvenience, pain, or other side-effect losses). Evangelism motivators that liken the Christian who does not witness to a doctor who withholds treatment from a dying person, argue from the same moral stage.

Middle-Level Illustrations

Identification is the key factor in Conventional morality's stage 3. "Christ Brought Me Out" makes the point that it takes one (addict's example) to save one (another addict). This is Young Life's "secondary identification" principle. The inquirer first must identify with the Christian at some point: athletes with athletes, musicians with musicians, addicts with addicts; then, he or she moves from the secondary hero or model to the primary one, Christ.

In social development Conventional Level Christians are more advanced than Preconventional persons who are *personally* escaping punishment or achieving reward: yes, Conventionals are getting their reward too, but in the context of and through other Christians. These concrete examples become powerful determiners of what they are committed to and how they live out that commitment. It is a "group faith" somewhat like Israel's faith, which was conceived of as more communal than individual.

Illustrations about "doing as Jesus would do" in the working out of one's salvation fit this frame of mind. One tells of a blind man who was trying to work his way through a railroad passenger car. The conductor saw him, found out his destination, and said, "Put your hands on my back . . . hold on and I will lead you safely where you want to go."[8] For these people, showing or explaining by concrete example is more effective than abstract explanation or illustration.

The advanced phase of Conventional morality, stage 4, is that of law and order. "Justice and Love" is a typical illustration of the legal and substitutionary understandings of the atonement. Here the father shares the absolute and legally required punishment, the loss of two eyes—an analogy to God the Father and Son. A similar illustration is credited to P. T. Forsyth, a British theologian. Shamel, the leader of guerillas fighting the Czar, hears of stealing going on among his group. Unless it is checked, their unity will crumble and their cause, if not their lives, will be lost. Shamel legislates the penalty of one hundred lashes for theft and, to his shock, the thief turns out to be his mother. After some soul-searching he concludes that the penalty must be exacted, but after several lashes, Shamel steps into his mother's place to receive the lashing because of his love for her.[9] These are "elegant" illustrations in that they appear to balance God's love and his holiness. Neither is circumvented.

By substitution of the just for the unjust in suffering, the claims of justice and mercy are both satisfied.

Upper-Level Illustrations

"The Scope of Salvation" highlights stage 5, the earliest one at the Postconventional moral Level. Walter Rauschenbusch, who said that "There are two great entities in human life, the human soul and the human race, and religion is to save both," was an advocate of the "social gospel." Instead of just trying to raise up the downtrodden, he also tried to keep them from being knocked over in the first place. This put him in conflict with those who, through the legal, economic, political, and other structures, were destroying the "quality of (the downtrodden's) life." If God loves the world as a whole, then he requires special zeal for justice from those most able to bring in an equitable social order. The Scriptures picture the perfect kingdom and city in which all the structures and forces which cause people to mourn, be fearful, starve, be ill, unjustly imprisoned, ill-housed, and improperly clothed, etc., have been wiped out. Thus, salvation also means the liberation of persons from every dehumanizing force (using Jesus' humanity as the standard) in the world, individually *and* collectively.

The logical conclusion of this position is a matter of intense struggle among Christians today. Dr. Miguez-Bonino, President of Union Theological Seminary in Argentina, points out that most Protestants who are concerned with social problems tend to ally themselves, in Argentina, Uruguay, Chile, and part of Brazil, with small "pure" center-socialist parties. The problem is that these parties, which are so comfortable to Christians of Puritan heritage, have little or no power. Thus, many younger and some older Christians are choosing violence as a Christian course of action. He offers us the illustration of Camilo Torres, a Colombian priest and sociologist, who died in guerilla warfare. Raised in the Roman Catholic Thomistic belief that "faith is only effective through love," Camilo Torres concluded that in his country the only effective love (in terms of clothing the naked and feeding the poor, etc.) was revolutionary love, literally. His life and death were testimonies to this logical conclusion which assumes that salvation is more than individual; it is social, structural, and collective.[10]

"The Call from Beyond" is quoted by J. A. T. Robinson in his book *In the End God*. It was written by Nikos Kazantzakis as part of his autobiography, *Report to Greco*. Robinson asserts that if we are going to see God, it'll be in our lives and experiences, not in some ethereal realm. What we see from Robinson's perspective is that progressive Force moving irregularly but surely to unite everything in himself. Thus, the focus of faith is in joining in and celebrating God's every move toward what others call "liberation"—liberation from every pseudo-God to God who is one or two steps ahead of humankind calling and leading it forward to the new eon, the kingdom of God aborning.[11]

Observations on Illustrations

One thesis in this book is that there are different moral Levels, motivations, and understandings of salvation. Because morality grows out of people's living together at different ages and stages of cultural and intellectual development, it's to be expected that life-in-general is a large pool from which to draw meaningful illustrative material.

Illustrations often give the appearance of proving the truth of something the speaker is saying because they ring true to life. Perhaps that's why those sermons that consist of one or two assertions or Biblical interpretations, ten or twelve picturesque and emotionally grabbing illustrations mixed throughout, and a poem at the end have such emotional force. But be not deceived, however well a story illustrates a point, it is worthless logically unless the point itself is valid.

Take the classic about the priest who chatted with three men working on a new church. He asked each, "What are you doing?" The first said, "Earning a living," the second, "Laying stone," and the third, "Building a great cathedral." The last person's remark has often been used to illustrate a proper concept of Christian vocation—we are participating in building some part of God's grand design. That's a stage 3 or 4 argument. However, this illustration has been criticized from those with a stage 5 orientation. The person who is caught "in the system," like the industrial workers who are exposed to unjust health hazards, may be simply surviving, "earning a living."[12] His dignity is that he is supporting his family, not that he is building anything great. So illustrations don't interpret themselves; people with a moral framework select and explain them to make their points.

Different types of illustrations seem to fit the different Levels best. Level I's usually have to do with good or bad in terms of pain or pleasure—we all know about those experiences though some of us consider higher values more important. Stage 3 or Level II uses model and group-loyalty experiences to present Christ as our great example to whom we should give ultimate loyalty. Soldiers dying for their comrades or suffering to serve their leader—anything that makes personal factors secondary to group welfare, the leader's way of life, or "The Cause" fits this category. One such illustration I've heard is about an elderly sailor who was sitting on the dock with his buddies. The friends were teasing him because even though he'd sailed for many years (under Sir Francis

Drake or someone else we studied about in history), he was as poor as the rest of them. His retort was, "Yes, I don't have any more than any of you and I've got to admit that I've been hungry, cold, frightened, and even shipwrecked. But, this one thing I know, I've sailed with the greatest captain who ever sailed the seas." What is moving to stage 3 folks is banal and ethically manipulative to the stage 5 person.

Stage 4's law and order appeal uses legal imagery, but any other kind of quantitative or sequential experience will do. Quite often "natural laws" are used to illustrate God's laws, the typical point being that people don't, for instance, break the law of gravity but get broken when they defy it. That understanding of "law" doesn't fit the philosophy of science (laws are our best description of how things appear to happen), but it makes sense to stage 4 thinking in which the utter necessity of rules for social living is greatly appreciated. Diagrams (Campus Crusade uses these frequently) and mechanical illustrations enable the evangelist to argue sequentially (like an analogue computer): "if this, then this, and then this, etc." Since the left hemisphere of our brain thinks this way and controls our speech (and is given 90% or more of our education), it is easy to see why this "systematic theology" with logical illustrations is so dominant in the Western world.

Postconventional illustrations most often come from complex interpersonal relations, that is, those situations in which several or many persons are interrelated. For instance, I believe it was Reinhold Niebuhr who told of a newsboy who, during the Depression, wanted to follow the Golden Rule and also support his mother. If he beat his fellow newsboys to the best corner, he sold more papers, and he and his mother ate, *but* some other newsboy and his mother did not. This awareness of the interrelatedness of all people justifies a passion to change unjust "systems" which give Christians no elegant solution (like the king who shared the punishment with his son), but the choice of who gets hurt more. With the awareness that systems break people, good and bad ones, it follows that these stage 5 Christians would "see" and emphasize the Bible's teaching that "principalities and powers" must come under the rule of God. Also, since the legal view of the atonement, like most court cases, can deal with people only one by one (or by "classes" of offenses), it has little if anything to say to the complexities of life. The argument of stage 4 legalism has always been, "save individuals individually and they will remake society." The historical evidence appears (to me) to be against that, as the slavery issue and the desegregation situations illustrate. Furthermore, just as Hitler's regime set up society so that no individual felt responsible for, or able to change, the "Jewish solution," so our society's complexities overwhelm most of us who must make ethical decisions with limited information we cannot trust. Stage 5

Christians think back to the days when they could say, "If I have offended any*one* today, please forgive me, God" with nostalgia. Today they know they have participated in the hurt of multitudes by not fighting against unjust laws they don't know about or understand, by some of the investments of the insurance companies who have sold them policies, etc.

My opinion is that stage 5 illustrations are not nearly as plentiful as those that point out the oversimplification of stage 4 thinking about salvation and morality. That's the nature of the beast.

I believe that all stage 6 illustrations are "intuitive." They are the product of the non-logical right hemisphere of the brain which deals with whole situations all at once (since they can't be broken down into a sequence without distorting them). It is the hemisphere that artists, musicians, and poets (who use much picture language) and other "feminine," intuitive, and Eastern type folks develop. It's a qualitatively different way of thinking. Therefore, "myth," "symbol," "celebration," "mystic," are important words. Perhaps this anti-legalistic slogan best captures it: "Life is a mystery to be lived, not a problem to be solved."

Songs of Salvation: Yesteryear's Music for Yesterday's Faith

> . . . some to church repair,
> Not for doctrine, but the music there.
>
> Alexander Pope, "An Essay on Criticism"

Jesus loves me, this I know,
For the Bible tells me so;
Little ones to him belong,
They are weak, but he is strong.

Jesus loves me—he who died,
Heaven's gate to open wide;
He will wash away my sin,
Let his little child come in.

Jesus loves me, loves me still,
Though I'm very weak and ill;
From his shining throne on high,
Comes to watch me where I lie.

Jesus loves me—he will stay
Close beside me all the way,
Then his little child will take
Up to heaven for his dear sake.

A Hymn Reflects Theology

When St. Theresa read the *Confessions* of Augustine she observed, "I see myself in them reflected." This concept is the classic test of art—does it mirror or indirectly reveal the real life and faith of every man and woman?

But art also reflects culture. If we want to find out what a particular people who lived in a certain place and time believed, we can see it reflected in their art: literature, poetry, music, painting, architecture, etc. Religious music is an art form. It expresses the theological convictions of the subculture that gave it birth. Thus, "Jesus Loves Me" reflects a time, a place, and a subculture: 1860s, America, evangelical Christianity. It was a time when parents took seriously the petition in the baptismal prayer for infants, "bring him safely through the perils of childhood," because many children never made it.[1] It was a time in which Sunday School evangelism was flourishing and its evangelists, like Lewis Tappan, stated unashamedly, "You ask why I cannot keep my religion to myself? I will tell you, my dear brother. Because I see you are in danger of eternal damnation."[2] As the times changed the "morbid" verses were dropped, but the song stuck. It is still the one song most associated with the Sunday school in evangelical circles. The song *reflects* the applied *theology* of the 1860s and it continues (in altered form) because . . .

A Hymn Is Also Reflex Theology

A "reflex" is a response controlled by the autonomic nervous system. You cannot control it directly. Just try to keep your leg from jumping when the doctor strikes it with the rubber hammer if you question this principle. Emotions too are reflex-like responses which get paired with persons, places, things, etc. After you've been to a great restaurant several times, simply thinking about it can cause you to get that good feeling inside and, like Pavlov's dog, salivate.

Music is one powerful "conditioned stimulus." Persons who were "soundly converted" when they sang "Almost Persuaded" will probably always feel some of those same emotions every time they sing or hear it. A whole segment of America and even the world had feelings of intense sadness associated with the Navy Hymn, "Eternal Father, Strong to Save," because it was played repeatedly at President Kennedy's funeral procession by the military band. Afterwards, every time they heard it they probably felt sad even though they couldn't remember why. Thus, even though the death-fixated stanzas of "Jesus Loves Me" are eliminated, the music and chorus trigger the feelings of childhood in Sunday school for adults of all ages who grew up singing this song. These feelings can be good or bad, strong or weak.

When a congregation demands the "old" hymns, they aren't referring to those written the longest time ago. They want the hymns that they enjoyed as they grew up, often regardless of the theology of the text. Hymns reflect the theology of the time and situation of their writing, but by association they become the reflexes of future generations of Christians who may have outgrown the theology of those hymns but not their emotional power.[3]

The Theological Critique of Religious Music

Dr. Alvin C. Porteous is only one of many theologians, hymnologists, and church leaders who decry the bad theology or heresy in hymns.[4] In his article "Hymns and Heresy" this professor of theology and ethics attacked specific types of poor hymns. One type was the subjective hymn; here the worshiper's feelings and experiences are highlighted instead of the "objective" glory and grace of God. Porteous also condemns the sentimental hymn. In this type of hymn, the worshiper "gets familiar" with the God who is "high and lifted up," as is illustrated by the blasphemous remark of a movie star who referred to God as a "living doll." The escapist hymn, Porteous continues, is inadequate because it replaces human responsibility with a religion where God goes into hiding with the person to comfort and console. These neurotic souls should be roused, not indulged. Thus, we should be suspicious of hymns that center on "me" not "Him," "myself" not "Thyself," and "I" not "Thou."

This attitude is a familiar type of "high" church, theological, or aesthetic evaluation. If equal time were allotted to those who still enjoy "those" hymns they'd probably say that they found the "other" hymns dull, hard to understand, and lacking the rhythm of the old favorites.

I would suggest that a fairer and more sympathetic way to understand religious music of all types is this: each reflects the beliefs and style of its moral Level (and stage) with all the strengths and weaknesses pertaining thereto. However, we should remember that the moral Level of religious music is often *lower* than the moral Level of the singer if it elicits a reflex of childhood or adolescent experiences which were emotionally positive. On the other hand, people rarely like religious music above their moral Level unless the music itself attracts them. This attraction is most likely to occur in musical people in general, singers in particular. With the preceding ideas in mind, let us consider the music of the different moral Levels, each with its strengths and weaknesses.

Me, Myself, and I
Preconventional Morality
Developmental Level I

This moral Level operates at the emotional level: it stresses that which feels good now or later. It tends to be subjective and otherworldly, often with a survival mindset. What kind of art, specifically religious music, reflects this experience? It is the music of those who have been on the short end of life's proverbial stick. It may not be considered "good" art, but neither is much of the experience.

Consider "country" religious music today. Its ballads were "hurtin'

songs" because the poor Southern whites who originated it were near
the bottom of the social and economic heap and they knew it. The
pre-agribusiness sharecropper and the pre-union (or union-influence)
textile worker, coal miner, or trucker often spent his life just barely
makin' it. Medical help wasn't sought till the tooth had to come out (if the
moon was right), or the baby was startin', or "you hurt so bad you
couldn't stand it." Red dirt, white lightnin', and blue songs when his girl
was slippin' round were his trinity.

If that's what life was actually like, then the religious music of this
moral Level could be expected to be as "earthy" in terms of religious
feelings and rewards as country music's other songs were earthy about
everything else.

Angel Band[5]

> My latest sun is sinking fast,
> My race is nearly run,
> My strongest trials now are past,
> My triumph is begun.
>
> O come, Angel Band,
> Come and around me stand,
> Bear me away on your snowy wings to my immortal home,
> Bear me away on your snowy wings to my immortal home.
>
> I've almost gained my heavenly home,
> My spirit loudly sings,
> The holy ones, behold they come,
> I hear the sound of wings.

Of course, country music of all types has invaded the upper classes.
The college generation as well as many middle- and upper-class persons
have rediscovered bluegrass. The "Nashville sound" is even heard on
FM. As lower class people have moved up the socio-economic ladder,
they have taken their music with them. The tech school, college, and
skilled-labor jobs may take the boy out of the country, but they haven't
taken the country out of the boy.

The Negro spiritual also reflects Preconventional moral understanding. This music has been considered primitive, quaint, and even "good"
art, but never good theology. These songs of salvation were too otherworldly, too unabashedly emotional; but they were great to sing, especially when one felt "down." Perhaps musical as well as racial factors put
spirituals "in" and country "out" of good taste, but theologically it's
hard to discriminate between the attitude in "Angel Band" (country) and
that expressed in this authentic spiritual:

Carry Me Home[6]

While trav'ling through this world below,
Where sore afflictions come,
My soul abounds with joy to know
That I will rest at home.

Yes, when my eyes are closed in death,
My body cease to roam,
I'll bid farewell to all below
And meet my friends at home.

And then I want these lines to be
Inscribed upon my tomb:
"Here lies the dust of S.R.P.,
His spirit sings at home."

(Chorus)

Carry me home, carry me home, when my life is o'er;
Then carry me to my long sought home where
    pain is felt no more.

"Carry Me Home" appears to be a far cry from the assertive and positive associations now linked with the spiritual "We Shall Overcome." However, that civil rights rallying song had a peculiar adaptability; it could be interpreted at the Preconventional and Conventional moral stages. Black slaves could sing it as long as that "some day" was believed to be their reward in the next world, not this one. But the song was radically reinterpreted into the "our" Conventional mindset of the civil rights movement as the fulfillment of that hope in their time. The "we" now meant every "good" disenfranchised person, blacks especially.

Another source of Preconventional songs of salvation is evangelical Protestantism. Though many "gospel" hymn illustrations could be used that highlight "me," "my," and "I" almost exclusively, there are many others that can be sung, like "We Shall Overcome," from either a Preconventional or a Conventional point of view.

Just as I Am, Without One Plea

Just as I am, without one plea
But that Thy blood was shed for me,
And that Thou biddest me come to Thee,
O Lamb of God, I come, I come!

Just as I am, and waiting not
To rid my soul of one dark blot,

To Thee, whose blood can cleanse each spot,
O Lamb of God, I come, I come!

Just as I am, though tossed about
With many a conflict, many a doubt,
Fightings and fears within, without,
O Lamb of God, I come, I come!

Just as I am, Thy love unknown
Has broken every barrier down;
Now to be Thine, yea, Thine alone,
O Lamb of God, I come, I come!

This "gospel" hymn elicits a Pavlovian response to evangelical Christianity, at least in America, because it is frequently sung when the invitation to come to Christ is given in revivals or crusades. It is not otherworldly, but like "Amazing Grace" it balances the singer's personal condition, the "I", with the gift of salvation through the cross of Christ. It was written by Charlotte Elliot, who was reared in the low or evangelical Anglican tradition. This woman, who was an invalid, wrote it out of frustration at not being able to "do something" to help her minister brother fund a school for the daughters of poor clergy. So she edited *The Invalid's Hymnbook* and gave the income from the sale of this hymn, which was substantial, to help found St. Margaret's Hall, Brighton. It is a song of salvation seen through the eyes of a person with deep desire to help and to be relieved of her human misery. Perhaps the depression-associated inadequacy and conviction of sin are so closely related in this hymn that it says what thousands have felt and perceived since it was penned in 1834.[7]

A widow-senior-citizen received this letter from a forty-year-old pen pal:

Dear ———————,

Many thanks for the thoughtful gifts and lovely cards for Christmas and birthday. Your kindness is surpassed only by your love for your Lord.

I'm glad to see that you are still quite active going hither and thither for your family and friends. I trust that the Lord will continue to give you the strength to carry on as you have for many years to come.

My holidays and special day were very blessed and happy. I'm most thankful for *this at this particular time in my life, for I seem to be buffeted each day by Satan. The period of trying seems to be an endless one, at least so long as we are in the flesh . . .*

This letter appears to be the expression of one who has turned into himself and now needs a good dose of God-centered, objective theology.

However, this man had been paralyzed from the neck down for about 23 years and had spent all those years in an iron lung or on a rocking bed. From there he "witnessed" through spoken and written (dictated) correspondence. But he does get "down" and, like many of the Psalms we read for consolation, he is honest about it. The content of his letter is similar to Psalm 88. Perhaps the Level or aspect of salvation you see depends not only on *who* but *how* you are.

We, Ourselves, and Us
Conventional Morality
Developmental Level II

With this Level we move from an emphasis on the singular (I) to the plural (us). Whereas faith was formerly motivated mostly by personal reward, now much of its drawing power is in Christ-the-model and then, faith-the-system. "Our" Jesus and faith are the supreme values, first because they are ours, and then because the system of belief and practice itself is worthy of our devotion.

Consider how country music responded to the Postconventional arguments about war and morality put forward by the flower generation. "The hippies are wrong"—not for any ideological reason but because they don't think and act the way we do. Merle Haggard's "Okie from Muskogee," which sold over a million records, perfectly captured what many felt. In the verses the emphasis is on what "our group" doesn't do: use drugs, destroy draft cards, have love-ins, wear long hair, beads, or sandals. The chorus reiterates what "we" feel, value, and do:

> And I'm proud to be an Okie from Muskogee
> A place where even squares can have a ball.
> We still wave Ol' Glory down at the courthouse
> White lightning's still the biggest thrill of all.*

Country and gospel music react against threats to the way they interpret the Bible in a similar fashion: with assertions about the validity of "our" way of interpreting the Bible and, by deduction, concluding that the other ways are wrong. Songs such as "The Great Speckle Bird" and "I Believe the Good Old Bible" assert that literal interpretation of the Bible (or at least the controversial portions) is what *our* kind of people proudly believe.

---

*From the song OKIE FROM MUSKOGEE (written by Merle Haggard and Roy Edward Burris), Copyright © 1969 Blue Book Music, Bakersfield, California. Used by permission. All rights reserved.

While the country boy was singing about the Speckle Bird, his middle-class equivalent might have been found in Sunday school singing about the "B-I-B-L-E, . . . the book for me." The mass of moral stage 3 songs, though, would be about Christ(ian)-the-model. Worshipers would pledge to be "true" to and be "like" Jesus, to follow him or his cross anywhere, and to be counted among his faithful followers. Military images with positive, rousing music are common.

Onward, Christian Soldiers

Onward, Christian Soldiers, Marching as to war,
With the cross of Jesus Going on before:
Christ the royal Master leads against the foe;
Forward into battle, See, His banners go.

(Chorus)

Onward, Christian soldiers, Marching as to war,
With the cross of Jesus Going on before.

The higher stage of Conventional morality, law and order, is also known by its songs of salvation. "Faith of Our Fathers!" "O Word of God Incarnate," and songs about the Law of God where one finds salvation in the narrowest and broadest sense of that word are clearly stage 4. So are those hymns which express the substitutionary doctrine of the atonement.

There Is a Green Hill Far Away (stanza 3)

He died that we might be forgiven,
He died to make us good,
That we might go at last to heaven,
Saved by His precious blood.

There Is a Fountain Filled with Blood

There is a fountain filled with blood
Drawn from Emmanuel's veins;
And sinners, plunged beneath that flood,
Lose all their guilty stains.

The World, the Universe, ALL
Postconventional Morality
Developmental Level III

At the final moral Level there first appears an awareness of Christian responsibility for complex social problems. Salvation, meaning freeing, preserving, and healing in all senses, includes claiming all peoples and systems for God. Chesterton's "O God of Earth and Altar" illustrates this broad application of salvation. Its author was reacting to the Boer War, which he viewed as naked aggression motivated by the discovery of diamonds, in addition to the already known presence of gold, in South Africa. The "prince and priest and thrall" (politicians and aristocracy, clergy, and commoners) were bringing damnation to themselves by either supporting this policy or by not speaking out against it—the classic division of sins of commission and omission. Read this song of salvation as if you were an English citizen around the turn of the century when newspapers were full of conflicting points of view about the Boer "problem."

O God of Earth and Altar

O God of earth and altar, Bow down and hear our cry;
Our earthly rulers falter, Our people drift and die;
The walls of gold entomb us, The swords of scorn divide;
Take not Thy thunder from us, But take away our pride.

From all that terror teaches, From lies of tongue and pen;
From all the easy speeches That comfort cruel men;
From sale and profanation Of honor and the sword;
From sleep and from damnation, Deliver us, good Lord!

Tie in a living tether The prince and priest and thrall;
Bind all our lives together, Smite us and save us all;
In ire and exultation Aflame with faith, and free,
Lift up a living nation, A single sword to Thee.[8]

If Britain specialized in the sins of colonialism, America excelled in the sins of economic exploitation (including slums) according to hymnwriter Walter Bowie. His "O Holy City, Seen of John," is a reminder that God's redemption includes the ghetto and the sweatshop.[9]

O Holy City, Seen of John

O Holy City, seen of John, Where Christ, the Lamb, doth reign,
Within whose foursquare walls shall come No night, nor need,
    nor pain,
And where the tears are wiped from eyes That shall not weep
    again!

O shame to us who rest content While lust and greed for gain
In street and shop and tenement Wring gold from human pain,
And bitter lips in blind despair Cry, "Christ hath died in
    vain"!

Give us, O God, the strength to build The city that had stood
Too long a dream, whose laws are love, Whose ways are
   brotherhood,
And where the sun that shineth is God's grace for human good.

Already in the mind of God That city riseth fair.
Lo, how its splendor challenges The souls that greatly dare—
Yea, bids us seize the whole of life And build its glory there.[10]

During this period, the turn of the century, Mr. and Mrs. John D.
Rockefeller were busy teaching Sunday school and bringing souls to
Christ. The New York *Journal* and the Pittsburgh *Press* rejected Mr.
Rockefeller's stage 3 and 4 limitation of what salvation was and what it
demanded. From a stage 5 vantage point the *Press* said that "With his
hereditary grip on the nation's pocketbook, his talks on spiritual matters
are a tax on piety," while the *Journal* cartoonist depicted him teaching his
class holding up a Bible, while ticker tape gushed from his mouth.[11]

In stage 6, the higher level of Postconventional morality, songs of
salvation emphasize Christ's uniting all things in himself. The salvation
orientation is not the substitutionary atonement, but Christus Victor,[12]
Christ winning the world and the universe for himself, their ultimate
source of unity.

God Is Working His Purpose Out

God is working His purpose out As year succeeds to year:
God is working His purpose out, And the time is drawing near;
Nearer and nearer draws the time, The time that shall surely be,
When the earth shall be filled with the glory of God
As the waters cover the sea.

From utmost east to utmost west, Where'er man's foot hath trod,
By the mouth of many messengers Goes forth the voice of God:
"Give ear to Me, ye continents, Ye isles, give ear to Me,
That the earth may be filled with the glory of God
As the waters cover the sea."

March we forth in the strength of God, With the banner of Christ unfurled,
That the light of the glorious gospel of truth May shine throughout
   the world,
Fight we the fight with sorrow and sin To set their captives free,
That the earth may be filled with the glory of God
As the waters cover the sea.

All we can do is nothing worth unless God blesses the deed;
Vainly we hope for the harvest-tide Till God gives life to the seed;
Yet nearer and nearer draws the time, The time that shall surely be,
When the earth shall be filled with the glory of God
As the waters cover the sea.

Songs of Salvation: Summary

As we develop morally we move from feeling, to thinking, to doing; from personal subjectivity to group subjectivity to objectivity. This development can be seen in the gamut of songs of salvation. At one end are those in which God rewards the singer in some way in the present or in the future. In the middle the singer and his or her group affirm their faithfulness to Christ their leader, who has paid the just price for their sins. They elevate the Bible and its interpretation of that doctrine and aggressively move out to win others to this same victory over personal sin. Finally, salvation is widened to include the whole world and all its political, economic, and other systems. The worshipers sing their commitment to be a part of the war against social, economic, political, and any kind of injustice anywhere in the world. Who knows—maybe soon we will sing songs about salvation which will say that God's law and justice should rule space. These Christians at the highest Levels are sure that God is at work winning ALL things, peoples, and systems to unity in himself. The Christian commitment to this task, not to nation, denomination, or self, is the highest loyalty.

⑨ Religious Backsliding: It's Not as Bad as It Seems

He has showed you, O man, what is good;
and what does the LORD require of you
but to do justice, and to love kindness, . . .

Micah 6:8

O daughter of Babylon, you devastator!
Happy shall he be who requites you
with what you have done to us!
Happy shall he be who takes your little ones
and dashes them against the rock!

Ps. 137:8-9

"What begins life on four legs, lives most of it on two, and concludes it on three?" Answer to the ancient riddle of the Sphinx: "Humans." The principle in this brainteaser is developmental: humans increase their physical powers until the threat of aging takes its toll. Then they regress. Aging also takes a psychological toll. Nostalgia, which seems cute at first, merges into childishness, which is not so cute. When this return to dependency and simplicity happens earlier than normal it's named (not explained) "premature senility." When it occurs even earlier we think of it as a "breakdown" or neurotic behavior which, as most of us have observed, can happen in degrees from mild to severe and in time-lengths from short to long. The typical cause of regression to earlier forms of thinking and acting is threat.

This chapter asserts that there is another facet of regression besides the physical and psychological: it's the spiritual, and it can be characterized by moving back or "backsliding" in the stage at which we think of and act out our salvation. It, too, is a reaction to threat. In this chapter, four typical threats and responses will be presented to illustrate this point of view. Then certain Biblical incidents and periods will be offered to support the same point. The Biblical material is not offered to justify or excuse all types and instances of spiritual regression but to show that it is part of normal human experience. However, as the reader will discover, looking at these passages from a salvation-stage perspective leads to a different interpretation of Biblical material.

Now let us begin with the most difficult challenge to the living:

Threat #1: Terminal Illness

"No, not me, it can't be true." That was the most common first reaction to the revelation of terminal illness found by Dr. Elisabeth Kübler-Ross in her classic study of over two hundred patients.[1] Psychologically it's called "denial." The trauma causes the person to feel as if "I must be having a nightmare" or "I am hearing tragic news for someone else." Even after the original acceptance of the grim reality, the condemned may slip totally or partially into pretending that "it's not true!"[2] This may be the only way these people can hold themselves together emotionally. A sentenced person may plant flowers for a flower show that he or she most assuredly will not enter. Others may complete courses that certify them for positions they'll never fill.

Denial, like regression, is a defense mechanism. It is a way of looking at life differently (actually distorting it) in order to "cope." Another way of coping, which may occur when our defenses are inadequate, is psychosis. Dr. Kübler-Ross tells about a terminally ill woman who had gone through all the psychological stages of grieving. She had started with *denial* of death's reality and moved to *anger* at fate, God, and others, then to *bargaining* (if you'll let me live I'll do . . .) to *depression* and finally to *acceptance*, which involved an emotional movement away from loved ones and toward death. Throughout her illness she showed a determination to retain her dignity and independence. Her only reason for living toward the end was her compassion for her husband, who didn't seem to be able to face the prospect of letting her go. When she was near death it was announced to her that an operation would be performed which would extend her life for a time. At that point her behavior degenerated. She demanded pain-killers previously unnecessary. Finally, in the operating room, she became psychotic. For her, continuing to live in pain was a greater threat than dying because her emotional resources had run out. This "selfish" desire was inconceivable to her husband. He considered it a rejection of him.[3]

As contrasted with accidental death, terminal illness gives the person a chance to work through the stages of grieving. Usually these end with a totally selfish state of separation in which two-way communication with the living has been concluded. Bruno Bettelheim's definition of earliest infancy, when the self is all, describes equally well this last stage of life, lending support to the "circle of life" view that humans leave as they entered life, in infantile dependence.[4] I often wonder if this deliberate separation while barely yet alive is not what is implied in such deathbed accounts as this: "When Jacob finished charging his sons, he drew up his feet into the bed, and breathed his last, and was gathered to his people." (Gen. 49:33)

Thus, terminal illness enables people to unconsciously regress back through the stages of salvation. One's contribution to the world has been made. Then, one's provision for his or her family, church, community, and other institutions is made when the person's house is "set in order." Finally, good-byes and last instructions are communicated and the person completes the trip back to where he or she began it: in a state of complete subjectivity. Severing deep interpersonal ties with the living may be the normal transition to establishing relationships with the "dead" as well as coping with the trauma of dying. Recent reports by researchers, who have interviewed those who were clinically dead and then revived, tend to support this interpretation.[5] The defense mechanism regression is the return to a former, *then* appropriate form of behavior. The kind of spiritual and psychological regression we are talking about may be considered the return to a former and *now again* appropriate form of behavior.

The pastor who senses moral regression and understands its meaning is in an excellent position to help both the terminally ill person and his or her family. The pastor should be objective enough to not be threatened by regression and subjective enough to communicate a deep Christian concern. The pastor's understanding and support is what the dying person needs; the living need interpretation, an emotional "it's OK," and support for their grieving.

Threat #2: The First Life-Changing "Illness"

Many people get their initial knock down (but not out) blow from the first life-changing illness or major physical change. Included in these punches that totally rearrange our lives are such things as diabetes, heart trouble, high blood pressure, ulcer, epilepsy, and loss of or damage to a limb or organ. Such changes also trigger the grief sequence: "This can't be happening to me!", "It isn't fair!", "I'll do anything you ask if I can just have it back," depression, and acceptance, which is everything from the bitterness-hostility and "cross to bear" form of self-centeredness to the positive "Let's see how well I can live within this new range of freedom." Whether someone comes to accept a restricted life as the glass which is perceived as half empty or half full, we can expect that person to go through all the stages of grief.

We can also expect a regression in the salvation-stage orientation of the physically changed. The save-the-world type may shift her total concern to her children and/or parents. The man who was pro-church and pro-community may regress to being anti all those evil groups who are out to get "me and all the things I hold dear"; and he may enlist the help of "hate" religious radio preachers and commentators.

A good moral question may be raised here: is this backsliding always sinful? Is it invariably a regression from the advancement in people's faith and practice for which they are responsible? Perhaps not. It could be argued that the means God has provided for us to survive some threats in life is to fall back on earlier, again-relevant forms of salvation understanding and expression. In other words, if the psychological regression to more selfish levels of concern is moral at this time, and the spiritual correlate of that is a lower stage of salvation understanding, then there is nothing wrong with rolling with the punches *at that time*.

The person who fears a life-changing illness and then finds out that the lump was benign or the heartbeat skip was psychological and correctable may also go through all or part of the grief sequence. Ironically, if he or she is at the bargaining stage when the good news comes, it may be construed, as was Hezekiah's reprieve for fifteen more years of life (2 Kings 20), that God has positively responded to one's supplication. I remember a serious conversation I had with a woman in her early sixties who was dying of terminal cancer. She had had surgery, but it was in vain. However, she wasn't bitter. She recalled that when she had gone to the hospital about twenty years earlier to be checked for cancer, she had experienced the normal anxiety and turmoil: the shock, the anger, and then the bargaining. At this last stage, she said, she had made a promise to God: if he would let her raise her family she would not be bitter no matter when he chose to take her life. God had given her twenty years. Then, he "took" her life. There was disappointment, but no bitterness.

Threat #3: Middle-Age and Middle-Class Crises

In a study of middle-class whites from age 16 years up, a number of threatening perceptions peaked among those in their late thirties and forties: doubts about marital adequacy; regret for mistakes made in child rearing; a belief that it was too late for any more major career or personality changes; the elevation of health as the #1 concern; and a new awareness of time.[6] These characteristics reflect a time of excessive demands: children in the most expensive phase of their education; partially paid mortgages; partial professional success and reputation; etc., etc. In other words, there is an overwhelming load and precariousness about one's achieved gains.

Probably no other group has been more maligned than the White

Anglo-Saxon Protestant middle-aged, middle-class male. I suggest, from a biased perspective, that comparatively speaking it is one of the more stressful positions in our society. He has more to lose than his lower-class counterpart, but not the security, freedom, or power of the upper-class person. The pressure is lower earlier and later in life. His religious conservatism, meaning his failure to go beyond, or his regression back to, law and order stage 4 Conventional morality, is related to all of the above factors. His wife shares this unfortunate situation if she is a career partner or if she heavily identifies with her husband's success and failure. Parents are concerned that their children, in order to become respectable and responsible adults, soon ought to move to Conventional (middle-class?) morality and, in many cases, not move beyond it by getting in social causes and relationships embarrassing and hurtful to their (the parents') position. From this comes the observation that the idealism of stage 5 social contract morality is most seen in the very young and old who have, as they perceive it, the least to lose and the most time apart from the survival concerns of supporting family, community projects, and child rearing.

Threat #4: Aging

For the workaholic middle-class male, the gift of a gold watch at retirement must be the grand irony. Middle-class status is strongly career-related and so is the sense of purpose and meaning for the traditional male.[7] Thus, retirement often means a loss of meaning. This is one scourge better eliminated than shared.

The ideal retiree is the one whose identity or sense of personal significance is not tied to his or her job, family, or any losable thing. However, few are that emotionally and spiritually healthy. Many tend to retreat or become alienated during old age.[8] Again, in our society, old men seem to fare the worst, because they have the highest suicide rate, typically following a health-related period of depression.[9]

Since alienation is one of the two common maladaptations of the elderly it is no wonder that many express this religiously through a regression in salvation stage. I believe that what I call "hate" religious and ideological radio (that which is agin' certain things in a vindictive way) naturally attracts these oldsters. The targets are scapegoats for anger actually felt about being ejected from a place or status and the loss of physical powers and looks. When the elderly send part of their inadequate income or savings to such purveyors of spleen they receive a psychic satisfaction but their financial problems are increased and they delay doing what is most necessary: developing a positive Christian philosophy of personal existence.

Ernest T. Campbell sensitively leads his congregation in intercession for the last two groups mentioned here (the middle-aged and the elderly) in his prayer with a time theme. [10] He begins:

We pray today, gracious father, for all who are hard put to come to terms with time:

> the young, for whom time seems to go so slowly;
> the middle-aged who find themselves with too little
>   time to do all the things they wish;   .
> the elderly, who mourn the irreversibility of time and
>   live with a frantic sense that almost all the sand
>   has dropped.

Threat and Regression

The thesis of this chapter is that psychological threat often leads to regression in salvation thinking and acting. This reflex, it can be argued, is modeled on the way we react to physical threat. A heart attack is a good idea from the vantage point of the organism. It's a painful reminder, if it isn't fatal, that the organism must back off and be selfish, meaning to care only about itself until strength is regained. Then the person can begin to take care of family and, perhaps, community. To ignore this warning is typically disastrous. The question of whether or not every moral stage regression is ethically right was raised and left open. Some backsliding is acceptable to God: that is the case being made.

This case can be supported from the Bible—specifically from situations when the covenant community was under attack. Bible commentators have felt it necessary to "excuse" the lower morality of these passages or books because of the unusual circumstances. This, I contend, is intuitive support for the moral-regression-because-of-threat thesis.

The Rise and Fall of Old Testament Morality

When the children of Israel left Egypt, conquered and tried to hold on to the promised land, they believed a stage 2 principle best summarized in 2 Chronicles 7:14: " 'if my people who are called by my name humble themselves, and pray and seek my face, and turn from their wicked ways, then I will hear from heaven, and will forgive their sin and heal their land.' " This promise, set in the context of God's covenant with Solomon, reflects the mentality of the period of judges *up to* the establishment of the monarchy. The whole book of Judges is a repetitive cycle of how Israel was faithful, prospered, and was safe; then she forgot God and physical disasters and foreign invaders threatened her until God raised up a judge who led her back to faithfulness, victory, prosperity, and security.[11] In other words: these were survival times. This moral ideology is called the "Deuteronomic formula." In the American Revolution, it was "Hang together, or hang separately," and served them well.

However, when the Israelites were established and secure, and their kings and the rich began to take advantage of their own people, we see the moral stage rise. Elijah reminded Ahab that it was wrong for an Israelite, even the king, to take a neighbor's field: that's stage 3 and 4 morality. The great "social" prophets, such as Amos and Hosea, not only charged certain groups with lawbreaking in doing such deeds as putting false bottoms in measuring vessels and fixing scales to weigh to the advantage of the scale owner, but they also moved to Postconventional morality. It appears that the establishment had "corrupted the system" and the people followed suit: "like people, like priest" says Hosea (4:9). Elsewhere, though both groups had contracted to serve God together, the leaders first became hypocrites and then the followers followed suit. When Micah says,

> What is the transgression of Jacob?
>   Is it not Samaria?
> And what is the sin of the house of Judah?
>   Is it not Jerusalem? [1:5*b*],

his point is that those in both of these governments have broken the social contract, corrupted the system, and the people (not willing to be left out of something good) have joined in. And, I believe, the prophet is asserting that responsibility for corruption falls heaviest on the powerful, since they have the greatest effect on national destiny. The powerful are the ones who most control the system of taxes, appointments, legislation, and are most able to influence it to affect their own welfare, even at the expense of the less powerful. The prophets' focus could be on social justice or structural morality because these were not survival times. (Future destruction was threatened by the prophets, but the Israelites did not repent.)

What moral Level is reflected in the Old Testament *after* the kingdoms of Israel and Judah fall and when Judah's beachhead in the second temple era under Ezra and Nehemiah is in jeopardy? It is Preconventional morality, with a bitterness reminiscent of an angry old man.

Imprecation

"Imprecation" refers to a curse prayer which typically says: "May you who have hurt us get more than you gave us, real good, real soon." The imprecatory Psalms, such as the one quoted to begin this chapter, can only be interpreted in light of survival times—bitterness is what holds together the nearly extinguished people sitting in Babylonian captivity. The book of Nahum takes self-righteous satisfaction in the fall of Assyria, with no expression of concern for Israel's own sins in relation to the nations Israel plundered. It is blood-and-gore delight, as is the book of Obadiah which, in the words (appropriately) of children, is an "I got you last" declaration coated in the theology of God's special place for Israel. Here we have regression in moral perspective for the purpose of national survival.

If Cyrus the Persian monarch had known what the Jews would face in their homeland he could have said to them, "I have good and bad news for you. First the good news. Under your Davidic leader you may return from exile with my blessings [Ezra 1:3]. Now the bad news. When you do get home and try to rebuild Jerusalem and the temple, you'll wonder if the trip was worth it. The obstacles will be so overwhelming that your very survival hangs in the balance. Good luck!"

The Jews who rebuilt almost didn't make it. The local people "troubled" them; the Samaritans wanted to help rebuild the temple and when they were refused they attempted to have the provincial government stop construction; the Jews were more interested in building fine houses for themselves than in giving to the "church" building fund, etc. Nehemiah tells us that when the walls were finally rebuilt the workmen carried arms and stayed at constant alert (Neh. 4:17).

How did Ezra and Nehemiah unite the Jewish community against seemingly overwhelming odds? They separated them from their neighbors. The wealthy people's practice of marrying non-Jewish rich was stopped. Even established intermarriages were dissolved! Each Jew was enrolled and his ancestry was traced back to its tribal roots. What a Jew was was clearly defined: one who is born a Jew and is faithful to the Law and temple worship. Some of the prophets helped: Joel interpreted the locust plague as a sign of God's judgment, Obadiah focused their hate on Edom's destruction, Malachi (3:10) reinstituted the Deuteronomic formula of the period of the judges in a stage 2 statement that is often used in our church pledge campaigns:

> "Bring the full tithes into the storehouse, that there may be food in my house; and thereby put me to the test, says the LORD of hosts, if I will not open the windows of heaven for you and pour down for you an overflowing blessing."

Ezra, after separating them from paganism, tied the Jewish community to the Law and its chief exponent, the scribe. Israel was saved from the brink of extinction by survival-related motives: good yields prosperity for you and adversity for your enemies, sooner or later.

It is worth noting that the traits of the Ezra-Nehemiah reform are very similar to those of the successful sects described in *Why Conservative*

Churches Are Growing: absolute commitment is required; a disciplined
life including suffering is the norm; the total system of belief and practice
is not open to criticism; complete conformity is demanded and defiance
is punished; and the faith claims of other systems are never seriously
considered. The principal difference is that conservative churches engage in evangelism.[12] However, the book of Jonah exposed this Jewish
blind spot and the Pharisees are credited with a program of serious
proselytism by New Testament times.

The Revelation to John

In addition to the period of the judges and the second temple era, the
later New Testament age embarrasses the highly ethical Christian because of the moral regression reflected in its literature. In the early
apostolic time the church suffered from the Jews but not greatly from the
state. Paul, who found his Roman citizenship to be a kind of security
blanket, instructed Christians to pray for the state as God's servant.
Christianity, as long as it was considered by Rome as a sect of Judaism,
had the safety of being a licensed religion. The fire in Rome and Nero's
opportunism changed all that. The followers of *Christus* became the
object of increasing persecution, climaxing in the direct demand to
worship the emperor or be punished. Thus, the writer of Revelation
protrays the Roman empire as the servant of the devil himself and he
admonishes the faithful to fight for the survival of the faith. Even though
many will die, he reminds them that martyrs will have a special place in
the new age. Believers will have the satisfaction of seeing all evil persons
thoroughly punished. Indeed, all of the apocalyptic literature, which
includes portions of Daniel, Ezekiel, Zechariah, Joel, Matthew, Mark,
Luke, and the Thessalonian letters, emphasizes the final overthrow of
evil in a cataclysmic battle followed by judgment, retribution, and reward. The Preconventional survival Level, like every other Level, has a
strength and a weakness: its strength is that it enables persons and
groups to survive; its weakness is that it leads to ingrownness and hate.[13]

Transcending Threat

It would appear that nations or religious communities facing extinction as well as individuals facing personal threat regress in moral stage as
a survival reflex. Here and there we see some, threatened just as much,
who are still able to transcend it all. I remember hearing of an American
submarine captain who led his crew in a duel to the death with an enemy
destroyer. When the torpedo struck the destroyer the crew gave a cheer
but he snapped them into silence with this command, "Silence! There

are brave men dying out there!" The best way to win the game of survival is to "play it" but the one who transcends it remembers that it is more than a game. Dietrich Bonhoeffer set himself apart because he never focused on the punishment of his oppressors: he ministered to them as well as his fellow condemned. And our Lord himself, as his life was being taken, prayed, " 'Father, forgive them; for they know not what they do.' " (Luke 23:34) Only God is in a position to judge people and people's response to threat.

Part **IV**

Dreams and Visions

10 Prescription for the Ideal Christian

That you may be filled with all the fulness of God.

Eph. 3:19*b*

To the measure of the stature of the fulness of Christ; so that we may no longer be children.

Eph. 4:13*b*-14*a*

From the time older people asked us, "What are you going to be when you grow up?" there was planted in our minds the concept of *maturity*. We may call it "having arrived," "our prime," "seasoned," or a dozen other names which change with the winds of language, but the idea that a person develops to a point when he or she becomes fully what nature planned for is one of our common assumptions.

Equally common is the awareness that few people develop their abilities and powers totally. "Scientists tell us we use only a small percentage of our brain power," we tell our students who feel inferior. The "Human Potential" movement assumes that a large number of people don't feel fully actualized and would be willing to purchase help to become so.

Development toward maturity is also one theme in the New Testament. The Greek word *pleroma*, translated "fulness," is used in some of the letters to express maturity and other fulnesses. Pleroma refers to the completion of time upon which God has acted, to Christ's "fully" containing deity, and, as in the exhortation (above) for Christians at Ephesus to develop into total maturity, to full "spiritual potential." These Christians individually *and* collectively (as churches) are exhorted to attain that complete development because their problems are personal as well as interpersonal, doctrinal as well as ethical.

How Do You Think of Christian Maturation?

Most human thinking takes place with images. One classic way of imagining Christian growth is horizontal. On the left end in your mind's eye (since we write from left to right) you might see stage 1 in faith development and on the far right stage 6. Just as the needle on your car's speedometer points to a miles-per-hour number, so you might see yourself at some stage along that moral continuum. The farther over to the right the needle indicates, the more advanced your development. A more traditional horizontal image is the Christian life as a pilgrimage. As Pilgrim progresses, he or she moves from the beginning of the trip, which is somewhere on the surface of the earth or a point on a flat map, to some kind of destination or holy grail. The moral stage implication of this imagery would be to begin at stage 1 and move as quickly as possible to the stage 6 destination.

Vertical images of attaining the fulness of Christ also have a claim on human thinking. Anyone who has toured ancient religious shrines should be able to observe the striking consistency about the placement of worship sites: they are virtually always placed high up above everything else. Closeness to the deity, in primitive thinking, seems to be *up*. The ancient Jew went "up" to the temple, the constructors of the tower of Babel tried to reach the sky; the searcher for ultimate wisdom must climb the mountain to find the holy man at the top, etc. Moral stage theory can also be thought of vertically. The fact that Kohlberg chose to use the word "Level" in his model of moral development is indicative of a vertical mindset. Likewise, the growing Christian can be seen as stepping up from stage to stage to higher and higher Levels.

The danger in our mental imagery is that sometimes it limits and distorts truth. I believe that the vertical and horizontal images in all their forms tend to imply that (1) people function at one of the moral stages exclusively, and that (2) the educational ideal would be for us to get everyone at stage 5 or 6 as quickly as possible. Then we'd have the perfect society. Neither of these implications hold up.

Actually people can think at a number of Levels. Further, their ethical behavior does not necessarily correspond to the Level at which they argue. Also, mental limitations may preclude most persons from attaining the higher Levels. Finally, and this is the point that will be pursued here, *perhaps each of the moral Levels has a ministry to the other Levels*. This ministry is necessary because there are certain sins that are more likely to occur at each Level. The witness and viewpoint of the other Levels appear to be the best countermeasures to those temptations. That is why the multi-Level Christian community can be so productive: as in democracy's system of checks and balances, the strength of each moral Level checks the weakness of the others.

Let us consider what these "Level ministries" include.

The Preconventional Ministry

The earliest Level of salvation understanding has been criticized for its emotionalism and its selfishness. It's often childlike and childish. Yet Level I is primitive existentialism in the sense that it recognizes the aloneness of every person. Whether we quote Amiel who observed that "we dream alone, we suffer alone, we inhabit the last resting place alone,"[1] or some other writer more or less profound, we are stuck with the truism that we humans contemplate our own beginning, and our own demise. I think that this perspective is helpful as we think of the vulnerabilities of other Levels.

Conventional morality's hyper-identification is what makes good martyrs, bigots, condescenders, and others who've handed over their personal integrity to *their* group. Luther reminded us that each one of us must do our own living and dying—and each of us must stand alone for the choices we made. That perspective is a useful check on community pressure. The Nazis used group loyalty to divide and conquer their target groups in Germany as they gained power. To appease Hitler each group was willing to let him eliminate other groups, till nearly all the resistance groups had been wiped out and there was no more reason for the Führer to feign appeasing anybody. Later Hitler used each nation's willingness to let *other* nations be annexed in exactly the same way. After the war the German churches helped lead the founding of the World Council of Churches in contrition for lack of individual Christian responsibility.

Postconventional perspective—which rises above complete allegiance to any group—is able to see through a divide-and-conquer strategy. But that does not lesson the temptation for Postconventionals to indulge in (and rationalize) acts of naked self-interest. How can Preconventional morality say anything to check the willingness of one group to let others be sacrificed? Simply by affirming that each person *individually* must answer for behavior. This is the positive and negative aspect of the "fear of the Lord." For those who respect God's judgment of them personally, it is motivating.

A second Preconventional ministry to both other Levels is the inclusion of feeling aspects of faith. Stages 4 and 5 are very cerebral; moving from thinking to doing one's faith. Yet whole persons, that is, persons who acknowledge all of their being, acknowledge how they feel about their faith. In so doing they have information unavailable to others and can deal with their faith concerns in a (healthy) healing way. One of the positive contributions of the Jesus movement, lay renewal, and other simpler-faith movements is acceptance of how one feels about faith.

Philip of Macedon, the father of Alexander the Great, had a slave whose standing order was to enter his bedchamber when he first arose and say to him, "Remember, Philip, that thou must die!" The liturgical churches have wisely used this same point in their Ash Wednesday ceremony. On this day, which begins the lenten period, a traditional time of self-examination and penitence, each faithful member is to kneel before the priest. The priest ("pastor" or "minister") draws a cross on the center of the Christian's forehead with charcoal and says gravely, "Remember, oh man, that thou are dust and to the dust thou wilt return." These churches follow up this affirmation by using the pall to cover all caskets. It reminds believers that whether the casket is a pine box or 15-gauge copper, whether the deceased is the President of the United States or a poor, penniless pauper, God's perspective is in no way influenced by the many factors which so much determine our individual attitudes toward others. In an age when death is more painless and private than ever before, maybe death, "the great teacher," has something to say that all of us need to hear: individual responsibility before God! in spite of who you are and, maybe, especially if you're important!

Finally, the practice of the personal devotional life seems to me to be most related to both the Preconventional Level, stage 1 and 2, and to stage 6 mysticism. The focus is on one's personal relationship with God, spiritual sensitivity, having God reveal faults, needs, and opportunities via meditation and contemplation, etc. These do not exclude our concerns for others, but they assert that the power necessary for the stage 3–5 "Journey Outward" into the world comes only through the personal "Journey Inward" with Christ, to quote Elizabeth O'Connor's book title in reverse order.[2]

Conventional Wisdom: Level II

Conventional morality and salvation is characterized by a simple following of the Christian models of piety it accepts and a concern for correct ethical decisions and ordered behavior. And so it frowns on Preconventional Christianity's idea of worship as a show or a treatment, and on its impulsive behavior, which it sometimes calls "backsliding."

It reminds Preconventionals that Paul had a high view of the church, that he pointed out that we were all bonded to each other in Christ and should be obedient to our civil and spiritual leaders. For this same reason, the "situational" or "contextual" ethics of Postconvention's stage 5 gets heavy bombardment from Conventionals. Even though its "system" of belief and practice has no place for exceptions to the rules, it drives home this reminder: 99.44% of the situations we face in life fit the traditional rules. The principal problem is not that the solution is difficult to understand; it's that it is painful to follow: it's costly faith. Especially is this true in sex ethics. Sophisticated people use their brilliance to rationalize ways to exclude themselves from the normal rules of Christian behavior. Is that any less evil than when ignorant persons do something which they are later ashamed of but do it simply because they "feel like it" at the time? If Watergate taught us anything, it should have been that when a person continually uses exceptions to the rules for personal advantage, then it's time for a serious re-evaluation of one's life.

There is a high similarity between Pre- and Postconventional moralities: both are individualistic. Both can affirm the slogan "Do your own thing," but for different reasons. The Preconventionals do it because immediate self-gratification is their highest value. The Postconventionals can buy it because they see themselves above all groups, capable of judging them all and freed from ultimate loyalty to any. This individualism is why when college students typically enter the moral twilight zone between stages 4 and 5 they get "beyond legalism" in their faith and they can easily revert to crassly selfish behavior (stage 2), justified by the morality axiom, "It's all relative, so do your own thing" (stage 5).

When a person discovers that rules can't be perfect and that "the system" has often been used to enserf the poor with unjust laws, there is a tendency to ignore the debt owed to that community, as if superior perspective emancipated one from normal obligations. Let us apply this to the offering plate. Each year the average *per capita* giving of Protestant denominations is reported. The denominations with the highest giving tend to be those with a Conventional view of salvation and which hold the law of the tithe up before their people. On the other hand, some of the denominations which have higher socio-economic groups as their majorities, whose members earn far more per person, give much less than those denominations of the poorer but tithing groups. One explanation for this phenomenon might be that the uppers who view salvation more as social and structural give more money to other causes and so drain off what they might have given to their churches. There's no way to determine this one way or the other but my experience and knowledge doesn't convince me that those "other causes" account for the difference in giving.

The institutional survival (stage 4)–social ministry (stage 5) conflict may also be interpreted in moral stage categories. For instance, assuming that the vast majority of denominational staff people of my denomination (Presbyterian Church, U.S.) have been drawn from Postconventional orientations, we gain insight into the current funding crisis facing us.[3] Back in the late '60s and early '70s our Boards and Agencies were the inheritors of decades of stage 4 denominational loyalty: people gave more money than the church spent, and the various Boards accumulated large "reserves" for crises and other rainy days. In the 1960s the leadership responded to civil rights, the Vietnam war, and other crises with stage 5 social pronouncements, study materials, and program funding. At that point the stage 4 majority of the denomination responded in a way not perceived at the time by many.

First, even though giving, in terms of dollars, continued to rise, the real value of those dollars did not keep up with inflation and the expenditures which were considered necessary. So, the Boards and Agencies dipped into reserve funds for several years, and then had to face staff cutbacks themselves as their reserves dwindled to crisis levels. Second, the local churches and lower courts (regional Presbyterian levels called "presbyteries") began to increase their share of the dollar received and the denominational offices at the higher levels got less and less. The solution proposed and accepted for this crisis was the restructure of virtually all of the Boards and Agencies in 1972. By 1976 this move was deemed a failure. Other denominations have had similar experiences.

I believe that *part* of the problem is that denominational majorities are largely made up of Conventional people who value their churches and denominations as long as they do what they think the church should do. Their giving records have shown that again and again. When Postconventional denominational leadership moves in such a way as to lose the majority the reaction sets in at the offering plate. It's ironic that the reaction was delayed by the use of reserve funds built up during a period of stage 4 program emphasis. Postconventionals argue: "A church ceases to be relevant when it emphasizes its own survival and welfare above its mission." Conventionals respond, "I don't think we define 'mission' the same way but, even if we did, you can't do anything if you don't face up to the survival messages given by the membership at large *when* they are given."

Postconventional Teachings

The Post's ministry to the Pre's is very simple: "you're being had." Gibbon observed that in the ancient world the magistrate (power holders) always found religion "useful." Marx and Freud asserted that religion was a form of escape, a coping mechanism for those whose condition caused them to be frustrated. Paulo Freire perceived this when the effect of the U.S. Depression struck Brazil. His family suddenly descended from the middle to the dispossessed class. Fulfilling a vow he made at age eleven to do something to enable others to escape the plight he knew, Freire developed a teaching program which used as motivation for adult literacy this ideology: enlightened people are able and responsible to act in ways that will affect their own well-being, rather than just accepting their lot by "adjusting" to it. Freire's method was so successful that he was "asked" to leave his native Brazil in 1964 by the military government![4]

Freire's work is important because it illustrates that the ignorant (Preconventional people) can be taught enough of the complexities of

Postconventional social ethics to fight the oppressive system. And, because they have so little to lose, as compared with the middle class who have a piece of the system, there is often a very strong bond between the liberal learned (who may be wealthy) and the poor.[5]

The key issue separating people with Conventional and Postconventional views of salvation is just this: the latter believe that Christ wills them to take responsibility for changing every system, law, and institution that de-humanizes people. Dietrich Bonhoeffer put it, "it is not only my task to look after the victims of madmen who drive a motor-car in a crowded street, but to do all in my power to stop their driving at all."[6] On the other hand, the Conventional outlook is most concerned with individual salvation and personal ethics. It will help a human in need but rarely attacks the power or system which may have put that person in need. You don't hear many anti-smoking sermons in tobacco country! Conventionals believe that if you change enough individuals, the systems will change.

An illustration that makes this point graphically, which I've heard in several sermons over the years, is about a tired parent and a petulant child. The parent was trying to read the Sunday paper and the child kept on pestering her. Finally, at the point of desperation, the mother happened to see a map of the world that took up a whole page of the magazine section. Deftly wielding her scissors, she cut the world into twenty pieces and told her daughter, "Here's some tape, put the world together while I read my paper. Then it'll be your turn and we'll talk." And she settled down for a long winter's read. About four minutes later the little girl said, "Mommy, look!" Lo and behold the daughter held up the world, perfectly taped together. The mother was astonished and, hoping that she was raising a genius, asked, "Dear, how did you ever do that so quickly?" "Oh it was easy. There was a person on the other side." (She turned the taped sheet over.) "You just put the person together and the world comes out all right!"

As was pointed out in the previous chapter, this appears to prove the validity of Conventional viewpoint because the illustration is not only considered charming (by Conventionals mostly) but it is a perfect fit of the point it projects. It "rings true" not because it's true necessarily but because it fits. Furthermore, it's so easy to remember that it carries itself with Conventionals through the years.

However, some stage 3 and 4 Christians do respond to stage 5 social criticism directly. They do not just work at finding good illustrations which make their position ring true; instead they attempt to deal with the issues raised. These attempts take various forms. One method used by Conventional organizations, especially those that appeal to youth, is to redefine and use the latest "in" words from the liberal Postconventional lexicon. "Liberation" is a recent one, the definition of which depends on the salvation perspective of the preacher. An older one is "revolution." In Campus Crusade's *New American Standard Bible New Testament*, Bill Bright has a one-page introduction titled "A Call to Spiritual Revolution." It was written about the time the "theology of revolution" was in vogue. Bright makes a case for Jesus and Christianity as the most "revolutionary" force in history. In his one proof quotation, he defines the "real" social gospel by quoting Samuel Zwemer.

> "The gospel not only converts the individual," writes Samuel Zwemer, "but it changes society. On every mission field . . . the missionaries have carried a real, social gospel. They established standards of hygiene and purity; promoted industry; elevated womanhood; restrained anti-social customs; abolished cannibalism, human sacrifice and cruelty; organized famine relief; checked tribal wars; and changed the social structure of society!"[7]

Bright concludes that Christ "changes the heart of man. He revolutionizes lives and, as men are revolutionized in sufficient numbers, the world will be revolutionized—the world will be changed."[8] This is a very well-stated position for the Conventional Christian community. However, its validity is an assertion, not a proof. The reason: the statement is a tautology or self-definition. Bright does not argue with the liberals about the fact that all the powers and systems of the world need to be brought under the Lordship of Christ, he differs as to *how* this must be done.

When enough individuals accept Christ—then—the systems will no longer promote evil because the believers will change them. This is a great *Magna Carta* for the Crusade campaign to win the campus for Christ and then the world, within a certain number of years in the near future. It would be no threat whatsoever to financial supporters whose money is gained from those systems. It appears logically invincible because anytime a critic says, "Your evangelism strategy hasn't worked, the world hasn't changed," the answer can be given, "That's not because the strategy is wrong, it's because not enough people have been converted!" So what appears to be a direct attack on all of the devil's empire is just an attack on the tempter's rule among people *individually*. The Postconventional position asserts that when Christians *and others* exert enough influence—then—the systems will no longer promote evil because they will have been changed. This position reminds us that non-Christians also work to rid the world of some of the systems of evil God hates. It asserts that one of God's directives is to focus on changing the system as well as the people. It argues that the power-possessing minority is more responsible for changing systems than the powerless majority. To reiterate: "What is the transgression of Jacob [that is, Israel]? Is it not Samaria [the capital city]? And what is the sin of . . . Judah? Is it not Jerusalem?" (Micah 1:5) Postconventional's most penetrating critique of Conventional Christianity is just this point.

At What Moral Level Does the Ideal Christian Function?

If we think in horizontal or vertical images we'd be inclined to answer: "At the highest stage." However, according to Kohlberg, only Socrates, Gandhi, and Martin Luther King, Jr. have made stage 6.[9] I would suggest a different way of answering this question—one that demands a different image.

I think that ideal Christians are those who function in thought and, to a degree, in behavior, *at all moral Levels at once.* They are persons who consciously affirm that there are valid moral reasons at many moral stages for doing safe driving as well as many other things. They try to do what they do at the highest Level possible, but they are more concerned about responsible behavior than perfect motivation. If they can't tap any higher motive for safe driving than not getting a ticket, they don't permit themselves to drive carelessly, even though they may be able to afford many tickets.

There are several benefits open to this kind of Christian. The first is in attitude. I believe the condescension and suspicion between the different moral Levels of salvation understanding is a scandal to the church. By keeping in touch with all those reasons-for-believing positively we improve our chances of hearing and being heard by others who need our ministry. This gets us into a second benefit: effectiveness.

To illustrate: pastors may make it a point to begin their ministry at a church by preaching the substance of the Christian faith at Levels both they and their congregation can affirm. After winning the congregation's confidence, because they have identified with its ways of thinking, pastors can introduce the new Level and stage with far less threat because they themselves are ones who understand and care. This is, in the epistle's words, presenting "the truth in love." But if preachers flaunt their superior ethical stance, this attitude, especially at the beginning, may eliminate any chance of enabling the congregation to sophisticate its moral understanding about the further implications of the doctrine of salvation.

The adult educational program of a local church can express quite tangibly the need for Christians to develop their faith at the various Levels of salvation. The church can offer a range of elective classes. These can provide for those who wish to pursue: the serious devotional life; the case for the creed and the Commandments; and involvement in "the issues of the local and world community." These classes represent the three moral Level understandings of salvation, and each should be supported with dignity. Granted that people tend to get stuck at one Level, there is still no justification for disparaging these groups with labels like "emotional escapists," "barren legalists," and "self-righteous world rearrangers." This attitude precludes the valid ministry *each Level has for the other*. Simultaneous multiple moral Level is the ideal for the congregation as well as the Christian.

For a final benefit, I believe that ideal Christians (like multi-Level churches) will structure into their thinking and experience the complete range of checks against the temptations of the moral Levels. Think of the Christians who have lived out their lives in this way. Some, such as John Baillie and Walter Rauschenbusch, have validated their multi-Level commitments by producing devotional material, being loyal and eminent churchmen and passers-on of the creeds and doctrines, as well as being on the cutting edge of the most penetrating social applications of the gospel in local, national, and international affairs. May their tribe increase!

Another such giant was Dietrich Bonhoeffer. This German theologian chose to return to Nazi Germany to identify (stage 3) with his people and lead their fight against the Nazi nightmare (stage 5). Bonhoeffer, while a prisoner, requested permission and ministered to all sufferers including those on the weekly "death row" in Buchenwald. One of these was Molotov's nephew, who embraced Christianity before (stage 1 and 2) he died.[10] Bonhoeffer's poem, "Who Am I?" is (when you know the context of its creation) both Level I *and* stage 6 in its outlook:

Who Am I?

Who am I? They often tell me
I stepped from my cell's confinement
Calmly, cheerfully, firmly,
Like a squire from his country-house.
Who am I? They often tell me
I used to speak to my warders
Freely and friendly and clearly,
As though it were mine to command.
Who am I? They also tell me
I bore the days of misfortune
Equably, smilingly, proudly,
Like one accustomed to win.

Am I then really all that which other men tell of?
Or am I only what I myself know of myself?
Restless and longing and sick, like a bird in a cage,

Struggling for breath, as though hands were compressing
   my throat,
Yearning for colours, for flowers, for the voices of birds,
Thirsting for words of kindness, for neighbourliness,
Tossing in expectation of great events,
Powerlessly trembling for friends at an infinite distance,
Weary and empty at praying, at thinking, at making,
Faint, and ready to say farewell to it all?

Who am I? This or the other?
Am I one person today and tomorrow another?
Am I both at once? A hypocrite before others,
And before myself a contemptibly woebegone weakling?
Or is something within me still like a beaten army,
Fleeing in disorder from victory already achieved?
Who am I? They mock me, these lonely questions of mine.
Whoever I am, Thou knowest, O God, I am Thine![11]

Bonhoeffer was also a loyal churchman (stage 4). He speaks of "we Lutherans" and never forsook his ecclesiastical loyalty even though he fantasized a "religionless Christianity" (a very stage 6-ish thought). He realized the value of law (stage 4) but also saw and taught that Nazi law and order were demonic and had to be resisted; he himself resisted even to the point of being implicated in a plot to assassinate Hitler. He was a man for all stages. He was a man who had integrity in living out each of those stages, if we can believe his biographers. If the New Testament canon were still open, his name might be added to the Hall of Fame list in Hebrews 11.

1	2	3	4	5	6

Surge on to stage six . . . !

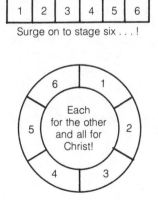

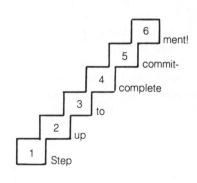

A New Image for Thinking of Ideal Christianity

Instead of conceptualizing development as horizontal or vertical and at one stage or Level, let me suggest a circle wherein stage 6, which represents individual commitment to the Ultimate that transcends all social contracts, merges into stage 1, our personal and immediate concern for feeling right with God right now!

I heard a psychologist, who was discussing tripping out, point out that the horizontal image of emotion was not accurate. In the center of the blackboard he put some symbol of the neutral state of the human. To the right he put increasing stages of positive excitement, interest, and feeling, with "euphoria" at the far right. To the left he marked off increasing stages of bad feelings beginning with a mild anxiety and ending with sheer terror.

Then he told us a story of his first canoe trip on the Colorado River. He was instructed to "paddle as hard as you feel scared." As he recounted his feelings on his voyage he began a little to the left of center with "strong specific fear." Then, after he got used to it, he moved through the neutral zone into positive excitement. Moving well beyond the class 3 rapids, and making it, he felt mild, then overwhelming euphoria. As the rocks whizzed by and the canoe barely missed them with the gritting of sliding of rocks while going over small falls with that fantastic whump and splash he recalled that he felt like a wet superman. But then a strange thing happened. As those boulders whizzed by he suddenly thought of their size and hardness and of his size and softness, and sheer terror set in. Then he remembered his instructions, and paddled harder out of terror and back into euphoria . . . back and forth again from terror to euphoria . . . from the strongest positive emotion to the strongest negative emotion like an electrical charge jumping from spark plug rim to point.

All I can remember about this man was that he was a seminar leader who was trying to give us some insights into the drug experience and that it was about 1967 or '68. But I shall never forget his point which I consider valid: emotion shouldn't be imagined as a straight line in any direction but as a circle with a small gap at the points representing the positive and negative extremes. People "flip" or "jump" back and forth across that gap. This may be analogous to moral stages 6 and 1. If you find this hard to believe, read "Who Am I?" again.

What Do You Do with a Giant Hypothesis?

Hypothesis: a genus of the scientific family. A provisional or working theory. An excellent pet (better than a rock). Useful: you can argue from it, explain with it, and suggest a course of action which follows from it. It requires no license in most communities but many are handled with great license. Most humans own a number of them though they may not always realize it.

This book is a giant hypothesis. It is a grandchild of Piaget's theory on cognitive development, the son of Kohlberg's theory of moral development, and, as I said earlier, the half-brother of James Fowler's stages-of-faith-development concept, which is receiving empirical testing at Harvard now. (Hypotheses tend to get extraspecial treatment at Harvard.) Fowler's work differs from mine in breadth and focus. He researches faith-ing (the process of thinking one's religion) in general whereas I have limited my focus to the faithing of just one doctrine, salvation. Fowler emphasizes how thought processes change religious thinking with each moral stage. I go beyond process to spell out how the *content* of "what I mean when I think of 'salvation' " changes with each stage, and I make applications for each stage.

Now, what do you do with such a giant hypothesis?[1] Answer: lots of things.

1. You Publish It

As the Revolutionary War was brewing, an eminent Virginian was asked to join the colonists' cause. He, being a very learned and careful person, felt that such a grave matter deserved serious and thorough deliberation. So, he shut himself up in his study and weighed, through the perspective of historical and philosophical studies, the rightness of our cause. After several years' study he made his decision, but by that time the war had been won.

That preacher's story (which I have yet to find in writing) is used to illustrate this principle: some decisions cannot wait until you are abso-

115

lutely sure of your conclusions. Many of us who have had research training are most uncomfortable with the partial care and feeding of hypotheses. But, unfortunately, one has to do one's job, raise one's children, etc., etc. So (and I believe that most folks operate this way consciously or unconsciously), publishing a working hypothesis is a good way to share the fruits of my mind and experience as well as an encouragement for others to evaluate what I have to say at this level of refinement. Perhaps it might even stimulate some scientific research, at least a doctoral dissertation. The risk of embarrassment at the weaknesses that may be found is outweighed by the good that might be done if the hypothesis is found useful by others.

2. You Suggest from It

There are four goals in science, each of which is built on the former one(s). They are, in order: to describe, to explain, to predict, and to control. A hypothesis is an explanation, after the fact, of what you think has happened. On the basis of it, you *predict* what will happen in new circumstances—you test your hypothesis. The ultimate goal, of course, if your predictions are accurate, is to set up conditions to influence outcomes.

My hypothesis is one of many explanations of religious development. It can be used both to predict and suggest actions to take in influencing behavior.

a. Suggestion 1: The New Minister

Let's apply it to the young minister, fresh out of seminary, in a first pastorate. Remember that in seminary the fledgling minister has discovered whole new ways of thinking about ethics, has acquired some higher tastes in hymns, and perhaps has built up a modest storehouse of "good" illustrations. However, at Modest Beginnings Church it gradually becomes apparent that what excites the young minister in illustration, topic, and hymn is far "too advanced" for the congregation. They like the "old" hymns and anthems, the simple illustrations, and to have the laws of God defended, not the difficulties in finding the perfect law of God for every situation paraded before them and their young people.

At this point the pastor has to explain what is happening. Perhaps a term from seminary comes back: "folk religion." That means the attempt of the culture to get religion to baptize its values and to use religion to manipulate God. If that is the minister's diagnosis of this congregation's problem, then the conclusion is to be diligent in hammering home the very highest Level of the gospel in sermon, illustration, and song—just what the minister has been doing. That is the minister's choice of influencing the situation. To reject this ministry, then, is to reject God.

The result? The congregation may reject both the ministry and the minister. With a "folk religion" explanation, the only other option is to "give 'em what they want."

My hypothesis or explanation is different. So is the course of action. The congregation is just at an earlier Level of moral and religious understanding. They haven't had the time to go to seminary and develop their religious understanding like their minister. The different course of action is for the pastor to find the stage or stages represented in this congregation's religious thinking, select sermon topics, illustrations, and hymns beginning at that Level and move on. Then they can get and move together. Note: the difference between this approach and "give 'em what they want" is that the minister begins, not stays, where they are. The integrity of both minister and congregation is upheld. A useful way to accomplish this is to involve the congregation in the sermons. Some ministers have feedback sessions in which the congregation and/or youth ask for clarifications about the sermons, or ask further questions. Others find out what their congregation understands by discussing the sermon's points in pastoral calling or at meetings. The most time-consuming but best way, in my opinion, is the practice of studying the Biblical text and topic with small groups before the sermon is written and discussing the effect of the sermon afterwards. After working through the congregation with a series of small groups, the pastor knows how the congregation thinks and if their thought Level is moving.

One of the laws of moral development is that people can understand and discuss one stage of moral reasoning *above* where they currently behave. It appears that we must do this for some time before we get comfortable enough to move on in our moral behavior. However, there appears to be some element of threat in doing this. People who simply want to walk "in his steps" can talk about a system of beliefs to follow but will have to do this for quite a while before "the system," *for them*, is organized securely enough to make it their faith home. The support and dialogue with the pastor makes that easier and, therefore, more likely.

My hypothesis, that faith understanding is a pilgrimage, was supported by three distinguished and high moral Level churchmen in recent publications. The first was an article in the *Christian Century* (Sept. 25, 1974). It was a critique of Bill Gothard's system by Wilfred Bockelman, Director of Communication Research of the American Lutheran Church. After pointing out what he considered the flaws and strengths in Gothard's brand of legalism, Bockelman concludes with this as his next-to-last paragraph:

Critical as I am of Bill Gothard, I remember that it is exactly through his kind of theology that I came into the kingdom. And I know that a lot of people whom I consider giants in the faith grew up on the same kind of theology, though, like me, they reject it now. It is good theology to be aware that God is not dependent on good theology, that he can work with bad theology.[2]

"Good" and "bad," when applied to ordinary theologizing, is a false dichotomy. "Earlier in moral stage development," but not "bad" in and of itself. That we go through stages of faith-development which were meaningful *then* but are outgrown *now*, the hypothesis of this book, is the experience of this author and many of his associates.

Ernest T. Campbell, pastor of Riverside Church, wrote the book *Christian Manifesto*. It includes his response to the "Black Manifesto," the demand that reparations be paid to black causes by whites for past injustices. The book is Campbell's attempt to spell out a balance between the personal-group (moral Level II) and social-structural (Level III) implications of the gospel. He recalls:

> I remember an afternoon conference in my study in which four or five rather well-known ministers who had established a reputation for sustained and courageous action in the civil rights struggle met to reflect on steps to be taken next. At the coffee break we fell to reminiscing about our beginnings in the Christian faith. Each man in that room, without exception, owed his start in the Christian life to some church or pastor of evangelical persuasion who cared enough about Jesus Christ to share Him with others. A central loyalty was cast that had served as a sheet anchor in the time of storm and a durable foundation on which to build an ever-broadening Christian life.[3]

Campbell says that both "sides" need each other: the personal and evangelical need the social and the liberal. I would phrase it differently. It is the responsibility of the pastor who has progressed further in faith-development to preach and teach at all the stages represented in the congregation up to and including his or her own. These stages should include the personal, group, and social-cultural aspects of the gospel. That is the way the minister, like God, can be a respecter of persons, touching every person's Level of faith understanding and seeking to unite it with the other stages.

The third publication is by Harvard theologian Harvey Cox. *The Seduction of the Spirit* is an autobiographical work subtitled *The Use and Misuse of People's Religion*. It's one of the few appreciative commentaries available on "folk" religion. Cox is an expert in the sociology of religion and hammers away at the "seduction" of the ordinary person's religious impulses by ecclesiastical, commercial, political, and other vested interests; he works hard to affirm the valid aspects of the "people's" religion. He seems to take the position that, even though every aspect of each person and each power system is tainted or corrupted by sin, people are not 100% devils nor are systems evil in and of themselves. Therefore, grace not only abounds in the individual's "natural," though partially distorted quest for God, but it also permits the power systems to be used at least partially to fulfill the will of God.

The portion of the book relevant to our topic is Cox's account of his baptism at age "ten, going on eleven." This is how he got into the waters of the First Baptist Church of Malvern, Pennsylvania.

> I got baptized myself when I was ten, going on eleven. That seems a little young, and in retrospect I can scarcely claim to have reached the age of consent. I can't say that I'd had a deeply emotional salvation experience beforehand or anything like that. I had not. I hardly knew what was happening.

After describing his training class and the baptism itself, Cox reflects on its significance to him later.

> I tried to be as nonchalant as possible about my baptism, even to joke about it as soon as I could. I even remember quipping lamely to the elderly deacon who helped dry me that I wouldn't need a bath that night. But I just couldn't pass it off as glibly as I wanted to. It made a telling impression on me. I'd be very sorry if in some future ecumenical version of Christianity that terribly primitive rite, so archaic and so incontrovertibly "out of date," were to disappear. I say that even though I was baptized long before I should have been. My religious crisis, when I agonized over whether I was saved, going to hell, and all the rest, came during my late adolescence. I even resented at that time that the minister and deacons had allowed us to get baptized, maybe even pushed us into it before we were ready. I don't resent it now. They were doing the best they could. They probably wanted to get us all into the church before we dropped out of Sunday school, which a lot of boys did in their teens. And with me, it worked. I did drop out of Sunday school soon after I was baptized, but I hardly ever missed church. I went, not because I had to, but because I wanted to. I don't know why for sure. Somehow it just seemed important. . . .
>
> Nothing is easier to make fun of than the sloppy, improbable form of baptism I experienced at ten, the awkward effort, complete with hip boots and warmed waters, to keep something of the primitive in a modern hygienic setting.
>
> But maybe we laugh too soon. Remember *your* emotional state at thirteen or thereabouts? Remember your need to deal all at once with anxiety and awkwardness, identity and faith, finding your way out of childhood, facing your own death, finding something to live for? Is it any wonder that nearly every culture in the world has devised rites of passage—initiation and puberty rituals—to deepen and resolve this perennial crisis?[4]

Cox's baptism was a "following Jesus" stage 3 identification, from which he moved to higher understandings of faith. As he looked down from a later stage, he saw that it was what pre-teens needed to go through about that time: he saw his former experience "objectively," as an observer. Like most of us he had mixed emotions about his formal entrance into full or adult church membership. He saw the establishment's (his parents', pastor's, and church's) desire that he make a Christian commitment and what may have been a premature, pressured, or manipulative strategy. Yet that experience, he knew, was meaningful then and, from his adult perspective, left a lasting, positive impression upon him. It was part of his-story (history), what affected what he was from that moment forward.

b. Suggestion 2: Local Church Youth Work

Many congregations perceive that the "problem in church youth work" is caused by the many independent youth movements which are thriving today. Some are even drawing foundation support because they involve masses of youth. In the meantime denominational youth programs have jumped from fad to fad (usually taken from secular sources), trying to attract and keep the kids. Hidden underneath these program selections is a repugnance to the stage 3 "hero" approach and to being too stage 4 doctrinaire. However, if most teens are at stage 3 (Christ[ian]- the-model) and capable of thinking at stage 4 (the system of faith), then it's time for the denominations that are in trouble to design a ministry that uses attractive Christian leadership and not be apologetic about it.

Most Mormon male college graduates give two years of their lives as missionaries. Wouldn't it be great if, for instance, selected college graduates of both sexes with some basic (maybe one summer) training in youth work could serve as home missionaries—youth workers in the local church and other ministries? Youthful idealism is there. Some denominations and groups tap it. Why don't others?

These youth missionaries could set up weeknight or afternoon programs for teens and even younger children (like the Youth Club idea) in addition to the traditional Sunday programs. What typically happens to churches who have used this approach is that their programs draw in neighborhood people and others beyond the congregation through friendship "evangelism." This approach does not ignore local church leadership. It just puts the burden of programming and time-involvement upon those called to give a portion of their lives to this ministry.

Over the years I have taught hundreds of students in Christian education courses. I have also interviewed dozens of ministerial students as part of a testing-evaluation program. This has given me the opportunity to hear many faith-histories. In every case Christian witnesses or models are perceived as significantly affecting Christian decisions. The pattern is especially strong in the adolescent years. The power of Christ(ian)-the-model is there. Why not respect our youth by providing it?

This can be seen as "manipulative psychology," if you want to state it in the worst light. On the other hand, it can be justified in terms of what the Bible teaches us about following "in his steps" and being a good example to the flock. Simply, it's just the way God chooses to work with people. My hunch is the reason many mainline churches eliminated this program strategy was their reaction against the excesses of hero worship in some independent youth groups and, more importantly, in the wholesale acceptance of group dynamics into church youth programming after World War II. Applied to youth work, Group Dynamics asserted that the youth group was to be a supportive fellowship, a "koinonia," led by adult "advisers," later called "facilitators," and would "enable" the youth to minister, with them, to each other. This was, theologically, conceived as the work of the Holy Spirit.

There is no denial that Christian youth groups can be very redemptive and supportive. But they can also be very destructive and even demonic. The adult leadership has much more control over its own behavior than the young people have of theirs. Hence, I believe that the leader's example should be at least equally highlighted with that of the supportive nature of the group. In moral stage theory, you work with youngsters who are at stage 3, using attractive Christian models who are willing to "let go" as the young people move on in their religious development.

c. Suggestion 3: Rewards

A third illustration of how this developmental hypothesis might be applied challenges the "best" Christian education theory about extrinsic rewards with children and youth. An "intrinsic" reward is the satisfaction one receives from just doing something: say, memorizing the 23rd Psalm. An "extrinsic" reward is the satisfaction gained "outside" of doing something: say, when Junior receives a New Testament with his name engraved in gold for memorizing the 23rd Psalm.

Since the extremism of the early-to-mid-1800s, when Sunday School scholars competed at local, county, etc. levels by memorizing Olympic portions of Scripture with scarce attention to meaning, the rule has been, "Learn what you understand." Originally this meant learning by heart the "golden text," a summary-type verse made part of the "uniform lesson." The uniform lesson, approved in 1872 and continuing to the present, meant that every Sunday school pupil in the world would study the *same* Bible passage on the *same* day and that in six or seven years the whole of the Bible would be surveyed. However, since the younger folks had trouble comprehending the adult portions of the Bible (Revelation, Daniel, Ezekiel, Song of Solomon, etc.), Christian educators launched "graded" lessons around the turn of the century so that whatever was studied could be understood. *Meaning* more than memorization was part of the sales pitch. It was argued that memorizing simply encouraged learning by rote non-understood portions in order to win a prize for yourself *or* to be like everyone else (personal and group motivation). The same principle was applied to attendance. Pins, stars, bars, class and school awards were frowned upon as pushing the right behavior for the wrong reason. Phrases like "quality not quantity" and "pure not ulterior motivators" are part of this argument.

Let's examine some aspects and types of satisfaction gained from the memorization of Scripture: say, the 23rd Psalm. First, there is meaning. This Psalm is very first-person: my's, I's, and me's appear throughout. The writer's simple image, understandable in all cultures, is that God is like a shepherd who cares for a sheep who's like me. Personal, moral Level I comfort abounds in the present and ultimate future: "I shall dwell in the house of the Lord forever." It is useful and meaningful to people at every age because we've all shared that stage of relationship to God if we've grown up in the Christian faith. That's *in*trinsic Level I satisfaction.

I would argue that memorization itself is also an intrinsic satisfaction.[5] We approve our children for memorizing a piece but they reward themselves when they realize that "I can say it by heart." Then they say, "Won't you listen to me, Mommy?" So you can't separate the intrinsic satisfaction of meaning from the intrinsic satisfaction of memorization. Mommy approves. The class and teacher at church approve. Tangible awards are given. These are all extrinsic rewards. Further, this can be part of a memory package of three Psalms, or the third level in a ten-level program of achievement of memory (with or without meaning) which the person and the class are expected to learn.

My contention here is that the reason behind the lack of Bible knowledge (and meaning of same) is that moral Level III adults have imposed their purer or intrinsic reward system on children and young people. By "purer" I mean the satisfaction that you have been true to yourself. The development of a "self" or identity usually takes us twenty or more years of life. Meanwhile we are progressing through the developmental Levels where personal and group satisfactions help in the formation of that growing self. A scout's set of awards may not all represent things meaningfully learned, but something has happened. The same with grades in school—they are imperfect indicators of what people "know" but they attempt to represent what our culture believes is important. Likewise in faith. Parents, church schools, and other organizations give tangible acknowledgments of achievement in what is considered valuable. It works because we sinners find it easier to do the right thing for the wrong as well as the right reasons: to memorize a passage because of what it means; the satisfaction of "I did it" and "You did good, kid!"; and the bar or the pin representing third level in the class like the other kids. IN MORAL STAGE THEORY the transition stage to Glory will be when none of us will need anyone's approval to do what is right except God's.

3. You Wonder with It

I wonder what the difference is between people who committed themselves to Christ when they were at a lower and a higher moral stage. For instance, in the late '60s and early '70s many young folks, involved in the social ministries of the church, decided to enter the Christian ministry. One such person and I had a long talk the burden of which was, "How do I minister to the fundamentalists and keep my integrity?" He had matured through four moral stages of development as a secularist and affirmed the Christ as he entered stage 5. The only thing I could suggest to him was to talk to his congregation and read religious material at their Level. The objective was to learn to appreciate how the middle Level of faith gives people the helpful control of Christian belief and example when they are tempted, and how, when tragedy strikes, the resources of the simplest stages of faith come to bear strongly. I think that this is what Campbell meant when he said, "Each man in that room, without exception, owed his start in the Christian life to some church or pastor of evangelical persuasion who cared enough about Jesus Christ to share Him with others. A central loyalty was cast that had served as a sheet anchor in the time of storm and a durable foundation on which to build an ever-broadening Christian life."

I wonder how many Christians, like Ernest Campbell, who have come through all the stages into a faith commitment which is *also* social or structural will be able to combine all the stages in their ministries.

I believe that the influential evangelical journal *Christianity Today* is now moving out to include in its perspective a concern for the renewal of social and political structures. Those writing with this point of view seem to be the black and foreign writers from less developed countries. Clarence Hilliard, in an article with this perspective, calls the evangelical who lacks a social concern a "Honky" and asserts that the gospel demands that the poor be enabled to help themselves, a distinctly social-structural view.

> The system that relates to the poor only from a questionable base of charity will never suffice, for such charity is designed not to liberate the poor and make them self-sustaining, contributing members of society (as in Second Corinthians 8:14) but to keep them in a state of dependency. New structures and new resources are needed.[6]

Clark Pinnock in his article on liberation theology shoots down the notion that the gospel is a-political:

> When we accept an alliance between the Gospel and the "free enterprise" system, we take a political stance.[7]

These articles indicate that even though evangelical American Christianity has been associated with a law and order stage 4 non-social outlook, it doesn't have to be. It can function at stage 5 social contract also. The fact that this broad view is now appearing on this journal's pages is worth watching because *Christianity Today* has the attention of the "silent majority." It also has a track record of being supportive and helpful to traditional-thinking Christians. I wonder if they'll be able to keep both points of view.

I wonder if "stage 5 moral relativism" is partially responsible for the alienation of the Boards and Agencies of some Protestant denominations from their people? Kohlberg and Gilligan define relativism as "the awareness that any given society's definition of right and wrong, however legitimate, is only one among many, both in fact and theory."[8] As educated people first move from stage 4 legalism to stage 5 (into substage 5A, social contract, utilitarian lawmaking), they often regress to infantile, stage 2 morality.[9] These persons reason at stage 5, but behave at stage 2. This was most dramatically illustrated in the '60s and early '70s by those who sang songs of social protest against all establishments but wouldn't unpack their electronic gear until a certified check for the performance was received.

Moral Level conflict appears to be at the heart of the conflict in some denominations. The leadership thinks and talks stage 5 social contract. Possibly people with that mindset are drawn to those positions because of their appreciation of power and the interaction of competing power forces. How they use their power becomes a problem.

After reading such books as *The Trivialization of the United Presbyterian Church*[10] by John R. Fry, I believe the primary weakness implicit at the stage 5 moral level, making yourself an exception from "normal" moral responsibility for some higher purpose, is illustrated when denominational leadership tells the church what the church wants to hear but operates by a private definition of words to lead the church where the majority does not want to go. I remember hearing of a sermon, by one of my denomination's late leaders, entitled "The Engineer's Got to Know Where His Hind End Is,"[11] the gist of which was that leadership should be ahead of followership but always in touch. But, being "in touch" means compromise. The leaders and followers both give in on their principles in full knowledge that neither is satisfied but that shared responsibility is what was agreed to in the social contract. In doing so they keep each other honest. But where "carrying out mandates" is mouthed by leadership but ignored in practice, you have stage 5 moral justification ("we're doing it for the church's best interests whether they're smart enough to realize it yet") for stage 2 behavior. After so much of this the person in the pew cuts off the money and/or joins counter movements in a schismatic denomination. How much better is any system which enables the stage 4 majority to not let stage 5 leadership make exceptions of themselves as they (the stage 5ers) point out the deficiencies of rigid legalism, especially in regard to how it helps to keep the *status quo*. Every stage has natural hangups or predispositions to sin built into it. It is not morally better than the other in that sense. Would that each of us would specialize in casting the speck out of our own eyes rather than the logs out of the folks' eyes in the other stages.

The other wonder I think about has nothing to do with the rationalism or logic of moral stages. I wonder how we "intuit" faith. The left hemisphere of the human brain is a specialist in logical thinking and speech. The right is the artist: it views wholes, is the expert in visual and auditory symbols. Many retarded people have limited rational processes and few of us have even fully developed what we've been given. I wonder if faith can be understood by the "silent" side of the brain in ways we do not understand. Maybe the medieval illiterate who viewed the mass and symbols learned faith in a way that we haven't discovered. Maybe, as some educators have suggested, we need to develop our artistic side in all spheres of life including faith. And, how would all of this relate to the appropriation of saving grace?

4. You Don't Canonize It

The purpose of a hypothesis is usefulness. If or when it isn't useful it should be modified or discarded, not held on to as ultimate truth. Mine included.

Appendices

KOHLBERG'S CLASSIFICATION OF MORAL DEVELOPMENT* AND ITS

LEVEL	STAGE
I. Preconventional (environmental reward and punishment)	1. Punishment and Obedience (present and personal)
	2. Instrumental Relativist
II. Conventional (group identified with gives reward and punishment)	3. Interpersonal Concordance
	4. Law and Order
III. Postconventional (autonomous or principled)	5. Social Contract, Legalistic
	6. Universal Ethical Principle

PERCEPTIONS OF SALVATION BY STAGES	BIBLICAL ILLUSTRATIONS OF STAGES
1. God My Rewarder-Punisher	1. Now the earth was corrupt in God's sight, and the earth was filled with violence. (Gen. 6:11)
2. God My Personal Covenant Giver	2. "If my people . . . pray and seek my face, and turn from their wicked ways, then I will hear from heaven and will forgive their sin . . . and heal their land." (2 Chron. 7:14)
3. Christ Our Model	3. Abstain from all appearance of evil. (I Thess. 5:22, KJV)
4. Christianity Our Belief-Behavior System	4. "A single witness shall not prevail against a man for any crime or for any wrong in connection with any offense that he has committed; only on the evidence of two witnesses, or of three witnesses, shall a charge be sustained." (Deut. 19:15)
Christ, Redeemer f the World's wer Systems	5. "The Spirit of the Lord is upon me, because he has anointed me to preach good news to the poor. He has sent me to proclaim release to the captives and recovering of sight to the blind, to set at liberty those who are oppressed." (Luke 4:18)
Uniting nt	6. So faith, hope, love abide, these three; but the greatest of these is love. (1 Cor. 13:13)

pmental Psychology Today (Del Mar, Calif.: CRM Books, 1971), chapter 17, esp. pp. 306-307; ucation, ed. T. R. Sizer (Boston: Houghton Mifflin Co., 1967), chapter 10; Lawrence Kohlberg and escent as Philosopher: The Discovery of Self in a Post-Conventional World," Daedalus (Fall 1971),

APPLICATION TO THE WAYS PEOPLE CONCEPTUALIZE SALVATION

ILLUSTRATIONS OF THE REASONING

1. "He who pays the piper calls the tune."
   "Speak softly but carry a big stick."

2. "Poor maintenance is too expensive."
   "Let's hang together or we'll all hang separately."

3. "My country right or wrong."
   "Honk if you love Jesus."

4. "When any man's freedom is endangered, every man's freedom is in jeopardy."
   "It's in the book."

5. "The president will uphold the Constitution, even the parts with which he disagrees."
   "We must play by the rules until they are changed."

6. The Bill of Rights, The Geneva Convention

BIBLICAL ILLUSTRATIONS OF STAGES

"I establish my covenant with you, that never again shall all flesh be cut off by the waters of a flood, and never again shall there be a flood to destroy the earth." (Gen. 9:11)

"For if you forgive men their trespasses, your heavenly Father also will forgive you; but if you do not forgive men their trespasses, neither will your Father forgive your trespasses." (Matt. 6:14-15)

Give no offense to Jews or to Greeks or to the church of God, just as I try to please all men in everything I do, not seeking my own advantage, but that of many, that they may be saved. Be imitators of me, as I am of Christ. (1 Cor. 10:32 –11:1)

But if there is no resurrection of the dead, then Christ has not been raised; if Christ has not been raised, then our preaching is in vain and your faith is in vain. (1 Cor. 15:13-14)

Do not be mismated with unbelievers. For what partnership have righteousness and iniquity? Or what fellowship has light with darkness? (2 Cor. 6:14)

For we are not contending against flesh and blood, but against the principalities, against the powers, against the world rulers of this present darkness, against the spiritual hosts of wickedness in the heavenly places. (Eph. 6:12)

They shall not hurt or destroy in all my holy mountain; for the earth shall be full of the knowledge of the LORD as the waters cover the sea. (Is. 11:9)

He is the image of the invisible God, the first-born of all creation; for in him all things were created, in heaven and on earth, visible and invisible, whether thrones or dominions or principalities or authorities—all things were created through him and for him. He is before all things, and in him all things hold together. He is the head of the body, the church; he is the beginning, the first-born from the dead, that in everything he might be pre-eminent. For in him all the fulness of God was pleased to dwell, and through him to reconcile to himself all things, whether on earth or in heaven, making peace by the blood of his cross. (Col. 1:15-20)

Notes

Chapter 2.
The Amateur Philosopher Who Runs Your Life

1. Material in this illustration taken from Charles Hampden-Turner and Phillip Whitten, "Morals Left and Right," *Psychology Today* (April 1971), pp. 39-43, 74, 76.
2. Adapted from *Developmental Psychology Today* (Del Mar, Calif.: CRM Books, 1971), chapter 17, esp. pp. 306-307; *Religion and Public Education*, ed. T. R. Sizer (Boston: Houghton Mifflin Co., 1967), chapter 10; Lawrence Kohlberg and Carol Gilligan, "The Adolescent as Philosopher: The Discovery of Self in a Post-Conventional World," *Daedalus* (Fall 1971), pp. 1051-1086.
3. *Developmental Psychology Today*, p. 316.
4. *Ibid.*, p. 316. See also Kohlberg and Gilligan, p. 1065.

Chapter 3.
Me, Myself, and I

1. Robert Perske, "The Theological Views of Some of My Mentally Retarded Friends," *Pastoral Psychology* (December 1971), p. 45.
2. Clarence H. Faust and Thomas H. Johnson, *Jonathan Edwards: Representative Selections* (New York: American Book Co., 1935), pp. 164-165.
3. Information from Child Evangelism Publications, Box 1156, Grand Rapids, Mich. 49501.
4. Box 1967, Seattle, Wash., 98111.
5. *Handbook of Clinical Psychology*, ed. Benjamin B. Wolman (New York: McGraw-Hill Book Co., 1965), p. 839.
6. *Developmental Psychology Today*, p. 273.
7. Harold W. Stubblefield, *The Church's Ministry in Mental Retardation* (Nashville: Broadman Press, 1965), p. 5.
8. *Ibid.*, pp. 54-58.
9. *Ibid.*, p. 61.
10. *Ibid.*, pp. 68-69.
11. Ernest Gordon, *Through the Valley of the Kwai* (New York: Harper & Row, 1962), p. 108.
12. Robert W. Lynn and Elliott Wright, *The Big Little School* (New York: Harper & Row, 1971), p. 40.
13. *The Book of Common Worship* (Philadelphia: Presbyterian Church in the U.S.A., 1946), p. 124.

Chapter 4.
We, Ourselves, and Us

1. Rafer Johnson, U.S. Olympic athlete, in *The Goal and the Glory*, ed. Ted Simonson (Westwood, N.J.: Fleming H. Revell, 1962), pp. 50-51.

2. From *Sharing the Abundant Life on Campus* (San Bernardino, Calif.: Campus Crusade for Christ, 1971), p. 117.

3. *The World's Best Books*, ed. Asa Don Dickinson (New York: H. W. Wilson Co., 1953).

4. Thomas à Kempis, *The Imitation of Christ* (New York: Grosset & Dunlap, n.d.), p. 15.

5. *Ibid.*, p. 150.

6. Alice Payne Hackett, *70 Years of Best Sellers* (New York: R. R. Bowker Co., 1967), p. 12.

7. Charles Monroe Sheldon, *In His Steps* (New York: Grossett & Dunlap, 1935), p. 1. (See I Peter 2:21, KJV.)

8. Francis E. Clark, "Christian Endeavor," *Encyclopaedia of Religion and Ethics*, ed. James Hastings (New York: Charles Scribner's Sons, 1913), Vol. III, pp. 571-573.

9. Émile Cailliet, *Young Life* (New York: Harper & Row, 1963), p. 13.

10. *Christianity Today* (January 3, 1975), p. 38.

11. *Young Life*, p. 67.

12. *Ibid.*, p. 63.

13. Young Life aims at the unchurched and the exchurched. However, its critics assert that if often takes churched youth away from their former relationships in church youth programs by becoming a higher priority of commitment in a world short on time and high on demands.

14. *Young Life*, p. 5.

15. FCA information brochure. Available from: Fellowship of Christian Athletes, 1125 Grand, Kansas City, Mo. 64106.

16. "God's Muscle," *Time* (May 21, 1973), p. 66.

17. *Ibid.*, p. 66. Reprinted by permission from TIME, The Weekly Newsmagazine; Copyright Time Inc.

18. *Basic Leadership Training Course*, pp. 1-2. Available from AWANA Youth Association, 3215 Algonquin Road, Rolling Meadows, Ill. 60008.

19. *Ibid.*, pp. 1-3.

20. David Ng, "Campus Crusade for Christ," *Presbyterian Survey* (May 1975), p. 58.

21. *Sharing the Abundant Life on Campus*, pp. 118-121. See also p. 41.

22. Edward E. Plowman, "Campus Crusade: Into All the World," *Christianity Today* (June 9, 1972), pp. 38, 39.

23. Carl F. H. Henry, "The 'Crash Program' for Campus Evangelism," *Christianity Today* (September 10, 1965), p. 42.

24. Dr. William R. Bright, "How to Discover God's Will for Your Life, According to the 'Sound Mind Principle' of the Scriptures," *Collegiate Challenge*, Vol. 5, No. 4, p. 30.

25. J. Claude Evans, "The Jesus Explosion in Dallis," *Christian Century* (July 19, 1972), p. 768.

26. *Ibid.*, p. 769.

27. Robert S. Ellwood, Jr., *One Way: The Jesus Movement and Its Meaning* (Englewood Cliffs, N.J.: Prentice-Hall, 1973), p. 114. See also Charles E. Hummel, "Inter-Varsity Christian Fellowship," *Westminster Dictionary of Christian Education*, ed. Kendig Brubaker Cully (Philadelphia: The Westminster Press, 1963), pp. 339-340.

28. Wilfred Bockelman, "The Pros and Cons of Bill Gothard," *Christian Century* (September 25, 1974), p. 877.

29. "Institute in Basic Youth Conflicts," *Presbyterian Survey* (March 1975), p. 54. Reprinted from *Strategy* (June-August 1974).

30. "Obey Thy Husband," *Time* (May 20, 1974), p. 64.

31. "Bill Gothard's Institute," *Christianity Today* (May 25, 1973), p. 44.

32. *Presbyterian Survey* (March 1975), p. 55.

33. *Ibid.*, p. 56.

NOTES

Chapter 5.
The World, the Universe, ALL

1. Barbara Ward, "Spiritual Bases of Development," *The Presbyterian Outlook* (April 7, 1975), p. 9.
2. Robert L. Faricy, S.J., *Teilhard de Chardin's Theology of the Christian in the World* (New York: Sheed and Ward, 1967), p. 171.
3. There are about as many definitions of intelligence as definers of it. The three "characteristics of highest intelligence" are those which I believe are most relevant to moral-social judgment in relation to salvation. I am most dependent upon insights from Jean Piaget and Lawrence Kohlberg.
4. *This I Believe*, ed. Edward R. Murrow (New York: Simon & Schuster, 1954), quoted by John R. Hendrick in "Opening the Door of Faith: Criteria for Evangelism," *Austin Seminary Bulletin* (March 1973), p. 28.
5. Ernest T. Campbell, *Christian Manifesto* (New York: Harper & Row, 1970), pp. 75-78.
6. Ernest T. Campbell, *Where Cross the Crowded Ways: Prayers of a City Pastor* (New York: Association Press, 1973).
7. Elmer L. Towns, *The Ten Largest Sunday Schools and What Makes Them Grow* (Grand Rapids, Mich.: Baker Book House, 1969), p. 119.
8. *Ibid.*, p. 120.
9. Barbara Ward, "The Christian Balance Sheet—Justice," *The Presbyterian Outlook* (October 27, 1975), p. 9.
10. J. Robert Nelson, "Ecumenical Movement," *Westminster Dictionary of Christian Education*, pp. 220-223.
11. Joseph Fletcher, *Situation Ethics* (Philadelphia: The Westminster Press, 1966), pp. 163-164.
12. Martin E. Marty, quoted in "God and Watergate," *Time* (December 17, 1973), p. 78. Reprinted by permission from TIME, The Weekly Newsmagazine; Copyright Time Inc.
13. From the Section 5 report, "Structures of Injustice and Struggles for Liberation," a preliminary study document prepared for the Fifth Assembly of the World Council of Churches in Nairobi, Kenya, 1975 and quoted in *The Presbyterian Outlook* (March 31, 1975), p. 14.
14. *Developmental Psychology Today*, p. 307.
15. James Fowler, unpublished paper, quoted by John R. Hendrick *Austin Seminary Bulletin* (March 1973), p. 29, and used by permission.
16. "Teilhard in the Trenches," *Time* (April 14, 1975), p. 47. Reprinted by permission from TIME, The Weekly Newsmagazine; Copyright Time Inc.
17. "Salvation Isn't the Same Today," *Christianity Today* (February 2, 1973), p. 37.
18. The developmental psychologist Piaget notes the difference between "assimilation" and "accommodation" in conceptual growth. The former occurs when a new fact fits one's mental categories (such as when a child is told that an aardvark is an animal); but in accommodation, people must increase the complexity of their mental categories so that all the old plus the new will fit. Moving from stage 4 to 5 demands accommodation. For a discussion of this see Paul H. Mussen, John J. Conger, and Jerome Kagan, *Child Development and Personality* (New York: Harper & Row, 1963), pp. 252-253.
19. Robert Mellert, *What Is Process Theology?* (New York: Paulist Press, 1975), pp. 11-12.
20. "Theism and Religious Humanism: The Chasm Narrows," *Christian Century* (May 21, 1975), p. 524.
21. Harold Lindsell asserts that Neo-Orthodoxy, through Barth's concept of election, brought universalism into the missionary movement, thus changing its prime character from evangelistic to socio-political. "Dateline: Bangkok," *Christianity Today* (March

30, 1973), p. 4. See also James A. T. Robinson's *In the End God* (New York: Harper & Row, 1968), chapter 10, "The End of the Lord."

Chapter 6.
Youth Evangelism: Its Power Is Its Peril

1. This resulted in a series of evaluative articles in the denomination's official magazine, *Presbyterian Survey*, on Young Life, Campus Crusade, Youth for Christ, and Basic Youth Conflicts in the early 1975 issues.
2. *The Big Little School*, pp. 35-38. The verse is Titus 2:9 (KJV).
3. *Ibid.*, p. 6.
4. David Ng, "Campus Crusade for Christ," *Presbyterian Survey* (May 1975), p. 61. From STRATEGY, September-November 1973. Copyright © 1973 by The Geneva Press. Used by permission.
5. Dean M. Kelley, *Why Conservative Churches Are Growing* (New York: Harper & Row, 1972), pp. 78-81.
6. *Ibid.*, pp. 138-141.
7. Cited in Samuel S. Hill, *Southern Churches in Crisis* (New York: Holt, Rinehart and Winston, 1967), p. 185.
8. Booklet: *Have You Made the Wonderful Discovery of the Spirit-Filled Life?* (San Bernardino, Calif.: Campus Crusade for Christ, 1966), p. 13.
9. Hill, *Southern Churches in Crisis*, p. 106.
10. *Young Life*, p. 67.
11. J. Claude Evans, "The Jesus Explosion in Dallas," *Christian Century* (July 19, 1972), p. 768.

Chapter 7.
What's Memorable May Be Irrelevant

1. G.H.C. Macgregor, "The Acts of the Apostles, Exegesis," *The Interpreter's Bible* (Nashville: Abingdon Press, 1954), IX: 238.
2. *Ibid.*
3. Marvin J. Taylor, "A Historical Introduction to Religious Education," *Religious Education, A Comprehensive Survey*, ed. Marvin J. Taylor (Nashville: Abingdon Press, 1960), p. 13.
4. Meditation by Wally Kennicutt for April 2, 1975 in *The Upper Room*. Copyright 1975 by *The Upper Room* and used with permission.
5. Nikos Kazantzakis, *Report to Greco* (New York: Simon & Schuster, 1965), pp. 291-292. © 1965 by Simon & Shuster, Inc. Reprinted by permission of the publisher. Quoted by John A.T. Robinson, *In the End God*, pp. 7-8.
6. From the sermon "The Satisfaction Christ Made," preached by Robert Strong at Trinity Presbyterian Church, Montgomery, Ala. in 1966 and contained in his *Sermons on the Person and Work of Christ* published by the church.
7. Quoted from Walter Rauschenbusch by Ernest T. Campbell in his *Christian Manifesto*, pp. 10-11.
8. Meditation by Josephine Abrams for March 12, 1975 in *The Upper Room*. Copyright 1975 by *The Upper Room* and used with permission.
9. Addison H. Leitch, *Interpreting Basic Theology* (Great Neck, N.Y.: Channel Press, 1961), p. 110.

10. "The Church and the Latin American Revolution," *Perspective* (Pittsburgh Seminary, Fall 1968), pp. 228-229.

11. John A. T. Robinson, *In the End God*, pp. 11-15.

12. A readable exposé of this is Rachel Scott's *Muscle and Blood* (New York: E. P. Dutton, 1974). One of her points is that some manufacturers find it cheaper (more profitable) to pay workmen's compensation than to make a plant completely safe. The relative costs of insurance-compensation and safety-pollution equipment may be calculated with a computer to find the most profitable ratio. See pp. 126-127.

Chapter 8.
Songs of Salvation

1. *The Book of Common Worship*, p. 124.

2. *The Big Little School*, p. 39.

3. Jack Renard Pressau, "Emotional Reactions to Innovations in Church Music," *Music Ministry* (January 1971), pp. 2-6, 42. Reprinted in *The Church Musician* (September 1971), pp. 46-52.

4. Alvin C. Porteous, "Hymns and Heresy," *Pastoral Psychology* (October 1966), pp. 46-47.

5. "Angel Band," text by Gaby I. Adams.

6. *Spiritual Folk-Songs of Early America*, ed. George P. Jackson (Locust Valley, N.Y.: Augustin, 1953), pp. 112-113. "S. R. P." are the initials of Professor S. R. Penick.

7. Albert Edward Bailey, *The Gospel in Hymns* (New York: Charles Scribner's Sons, 1950), pp. 182-183.

8. "O God of Earth and Altar" by G. K. Chesterton (1874-1936). By permission of Oxford University Press.

9. *The Gospel in Hymns*, p. 571.

10. "O Holy City, Seen of John" by Walter Russell Bowie. Used by permission of Harper & Row, Publishers, Inc.

11. Raymond B. Fosdick, *John D. Rockefeller, Jr.: A Portrait* (New York: Harper & Brothers, 1956), pp. 126-127.

12. Some other hymns couched in the Christus Victor perspective are:

"Welcome, Happy Morning!" by Venantius Fortunatus, 530-609
"A Mighty Fortress Is Our God" by Martin Luther, 1529
"Am I a Soldier of the Cross" by Isaac Watts, 1724
"Stand Up, Stand Up for Jesus" by George Duffield, 1858
"Onward, Christian Soldiers" by Sabine Baring-Gould, 1864
"Thine Is the Glory" by Edmond Budry, 1884.

Chapter 9.
Religious Backsliding: It's Not as Bad as It Seems

1. Elisabeth Kübler-Ross, *On Death and Dying* (New York: The Macmillan Co., 1969), p. 38.

2. *Ibid.*, pp. 38-41.

3. *Ibid.*, pp. 114-119.

4. *Ibid.*, p. 120.

5. Elisabeth Kübler-Ross, *Questions and Answers on Death and Dying* (New York: The Macmillan Co., 1974), p. 167.

6. See Roger Gould, "Adult Life Stages: Growth Toward Self-Tolerance," *Psychology Today* (February 1975), pp. 74-78.

7. Zena Smith Blau, *Old Age in a Changing Society* (New York: Franklin Watts, Inc., 1973), p. 156.

8. *Ibid.*, p. 152.

9. *Developmental Psychology Today*, p. 508.

10. *Where Cross the Crowded Ways*, p. 48.

11. Bernhard W. Anderson, *Understanding the Old Testament* (Englewood Cliffs, N.J.: Prentice-Hall, 1975), pp. 111.

12. *Why Conservative Churches Are Growing*, pp. 58 and 79.

13. C. Milo Connick observes the tendency to hate in Revelation (*The New Testament* [Encino, Calif.: Dickenson Publishing Co., 1972], p. 339), and Bernhard Anderson (*Understanding the Old Testament*, pp. 357-361) criticizes the Jewish religion of the second temple period for building a legalism and pride through what he calls a "bargain-counter religion," which we call stage 2.

Chapter 10.
Prescription for the Ideal Christian

1. *The Journal Intimé of Henri-Frédéric Amiel*, trans. Mrs. Humphry Ward (New York: The Macmillan Co., 1923), p. 335.

2. Elizabeth O'Connor, *Journey Inward, Journey Outward* (New York: Harper & Row, 1968).

3. "Doing Something about Organizational Crisis," *Presbyterian Survey* (March 1976), pp. 28-32.

4. Paolo Freire, *Pedagogy of the Oppressed* (New York: Herder and Herder, 1972), pp. 11-12.

5. An excellent article that distinguishes between the typical lower-class "Holiness Movement" and middle-class fundamentalism as to difference in moral stage behind their outlooks is "The Holiness Churches: A Significant Ethical Tradition" by Donald Dayton, *Christian Century* (February 26, 1975), pp. 197-201.

6. Quoted by G. Leibholz in the "Memoir" in Dietrich Bonhoeffer, *The Cost of Discipleship* (New York: The Macmillan Co., 1948), pp. 22-23.

7. *New American Standard Bible New Testament*, special edition (Mineola, New York: The Foundation Press, Inc., 1960).

8. *Ibid.*

9. "Moral Education," *Newsweek* (March 1, 1976), p . 74.

10. See the "Memoir," *The Cost of Discipleship*, pp. 9-28.

11. Dietrich Bonhoeffer, *Letters and Papers from Prison*, revised ed., ed. Eberhard Bethge (New York: The Macmillan Co., 1967), pp. 197-198. © 1967 by The Macmillan Co. Reprinted by permission of the publisher.

Chapter 11.
What Do You Do with a Giant Hypothesis?

1. A more theoretical question is, "Why hasn't Christian theology discovered these stages earlier?" Perhaps it has. Libuse Lukas Miller's *In Search of the Self: The Individual in the Thought of Kierkegaard* (Philadelphia: Muhlenberg Press, 1962), for example, devotes two chapters (7 and 8) to stage or "sphere of existence" thinking in the writings of Kierkegaard. The first stage Kierkegaard calls the "aesthetic." This means, according to Miller, "any manner of living in which the principle that one should seek pleasure and avoid pain is . . . the dominant, or decisive principle." The closest synonyms to "aesthetic" in current language, Miller says, would be "hedonic" or "hedonistic" (p. 156). This stage includes not only the comfort cravers but also those whose religious

motivation is aesthetic, that is, engaged in for artistic satisfactions rather than strictly religious ones, and also the social climbers who use religious involvement to get ahead.

Kierkegaard's second stage is the "ethical"—"a striving consisting of trying to embody somehow the highest good in all the essential acts of the person" (p. 169). The *time* element is critical in this stage. One must be willing to wait and work tenaciously for reward. Psychologists often call this "delayed gratification."

The last stage is the "religious," the one in which concrete and absolute commitment is made, such as that illustrated when Abraham was ready to sacrifice Isaac (186ff.). This is a complex stage in which awareness of the conflict between two "oughts" becomes a painful responsibility for choice, "pure" motivation as a moral responsibility is discovered, and the *relative* awareness of religious forms and doctrines is held as necessary while the believer is simultaneously aware of his or her *absolute* responsibility to the God who is ultimately unknowable.

It appears that Kierkegaard is describing salvation stages 1, 2, and then 3-6 in some very complex combination. Many of his observations about these spheres can be identified with moral stage theory. For instance, Kierkegaard has these stages as sequential integrations, which, when they are challenged and after some trauma and a "leap of faith," enable the person to go on to the next integration or stage. Kierkegaard suggested typical life periods when one could be expected to develop to certain stages. He also believed that some persons reached the ethical and religious stages earlier than others, and that others never develop beyond the earlier ones. Kierkegaard considered himself "old" in religious stage, in radical contrast to the girl he was to marry, whom he characterized as a permanently "childlike" aesthetic, two stages behind him. Finally, he believed that one could regress back through the stages under certain conditions (p. 157).

Kierkegaard's scheme is an ethical-religious one and should be expected to show similarity to my hypothesis. From this secondary-source analysis, I believe that it does. Other religious writers' "systems" may also show striking similarities to the salvation-stage hypothesis if explored. I think this might be an excellent dissertation topic!

2. "The Pros and Cons of Bill Gothard," *Christian Century* (September 25, 1974), p. 880.

3. *Christian Manifesto*, p. 8.

4. Harvey Cox, *The Seduction of the Spirit* (New York: Simon and Schuster, 1973), pp. 37 and 39.

5. It can be argued that we learn to be satisfied with ourselves because when we memorize good things happen, such as we can find our socks, pass our exams, or remember a birthday of a loved one. However, reality so conditions us very early in life (kids have socks, toys, and programs they don't want to miss) that for all practical purposes, memorization achievement is intrinsically rewarding—"I did it *my*self" (moral Level I) like all the other kids (moral Level II).

6. Clarence Hilliard, "Down with the Honky Christ—Up with the Funky Jesus," *Christianity Today* (January 30, 1976), pp. 6-8.

7. Clark H. Pinnock, "Liberation Theology: The Gains, the Gaps," *Christianity Today* (January 16, 1976), p. 14.

8. Kohlberg and Gilligan, "The Adolescent as Philosopher," *Daedalus* (Fall 1971), p. 1072. See also Ronald Duska and Mariellen Whelan, *Moral Development* (New York: Paulist Press, 1975), p. 70ff.

9. *Ibid.* and Alfred L. Baldwin, "A Cognitive Theory of Socialization," in *Handbook of Socialization Theory and Research*, ed. David A. Goslin (Chicago: Rand McNally, 1969), pp. 388 and 428, note 12.

10. John R. Fry, *The Trivialization of the United Presbyterian Church* (New York: Harper & Row, 1975).

11. Kenneth J. Foreman, *Christianity Today* (May 12, 1967), pp. 16-17.

Index of Bible References

Index of Names and Subjects